GOING INTERNATIONAL — the experience of smaller companies overseas

GOING INTERNATIONAL
— the experience of smaller companies overseas

GERALD D. NEWBOULD, BCom, MA, PhD
Chairman of Finance,
Cleveland State University, USA

PETER J. BUCKLEY, BA, MA, PhD
Lecturer in International Business,
University of Bradford Management Centre, UK

JANE C. THURWELL, BA
Consumer Marketing and Planning Research,
Philips Industries, UK

A HALSTED PRESS BOOK

JOHN WILEY & SONS
New York — Toronto

All Rights Reserved. No part of this publication may be reproduced, stored in a retrieval system or transmitted in any form or by any means: electronic, electrostatic, magnetic tape, mechanical, photocopying, recording or otherwise, without permission in writing from the publishers.

English language edition, except USA and Canada published by
Associated Business Press
An imprint of Associated Business Programmes Limited
Ludgate House
107-111 Fleet Street
London EC4A 2AB

Published in the USA and Canada by
Halsted Press, a Division of
John Wiley & Sons Inc.
New York

First published 1978

Library of Congress Cataloging in Publication Data

Newbould, Gerald David
  Going International

"A Halsted Press book."

  1. International business enterprises — Management.
2. Small business — Management. I. Buckley, Peter J., 1949- joint author. II. Thurwell, Jane C., joint author. III. Title.
HD69.17N47 1978 658.1'8 78-15729

ISBN 0 470 26493 4

© Gerald D Newbould, Peter J Buckley, Jane Thurwell

  Printed and bound in Great Britain by
  A. Wheaton & Company, Limited
  Exeter, Devon

Contents

	Acknowledgements	vii
1	Going international	1
2	The firms in the sample	6
3	The success of overseas production subsidiaries	15
4	The preliminary stages	43
5	The planning stages	69
6	The investing stages	98
7	Controlling the subsidiary	126
8	Lessons and problems	152
9	Overseas sales subsidiaries	179
10	Profile of a successful production subsidiary	199
	Appendices	
I	Regulations, policies and inducements, by country	202
II	UK exchange control policy	229
III	Questionnaire	232
	Index	241

Acknowledgements

The research was carried out while the three authors were at the University of Bradford Management Centre and acknowledgement is due to colleagues there whose abilities fostered the environment conducive to research.

In terms of direct help we are indebted to those senior managers who spent time with us providing the material for this report and in commenting upon the first draft:

M. A. Alexander	G. A. Jowitt
F. D. Biddle	W. H. Liversidge
J. Casling	L. O. Luff
P. S. Caton	D. R. Marshall
W. R. Cheston	G. L. Myles
A. Connor Wilson	R. Noskwith
B. Crossley	W. Reik
F. T. Davies	M. K. Rose
B. B. Dearden	S. M. Selka
P. Down	N. Styles
E. P. Foden	J. M. Tildesley
N. Fountain	B. A. Wallace
S. Fox	D. Westermann
J. P. Hawksfield	D. Westwood
F. Hicks	P. D. Wheatley
D. R. Hope	P. E. J. White
H. H. Jackson	R. I. Woods
A. Jannece	

Equal acknowledgement is made to those senior managers who prefer to remain anonymous.

Further helpful comments on the first draft were provided by Bernard Wolf and the numerous drafts were processed with unfailing spirit by Sylvia Ashdown, Debbie Zahar, and Caroline Newbould. Our thanks to these people for their help.

Primary financial support was provided by the Foundation for Management Education, and the Houblon-Norman Fund at the Bank of England provided for the travelling expenses. Without the support of these two bodies, the research could not have taken place, and thus the acknowledgement is a grateful one.

Finally the usual rider is in place: help was essential from all the above but, in the end, what appears is solely the responsibility of the authors.

Cleveland and Bradford
March 1978

1 Going international

Beating the competition is always satisfying; and beating the competition on their home ground is especially satisfying. This is widely accepted as true in sport, but it is no less so in business. During the interviews on which this report is based, the satisfaction of those managers being interviewed, who had challenged foreign firms in their home market and succeeded, was obvious, and even exciting to both managers and interviewers alike. Of course it is necessary to record as fully those interviews where the venture was a failure and those interviews, embarrassing for all concerned, where the venture was a fiasco. This book concentrates upon these differences in levels of success and failure in going international in the belief that the experiences of the persons interviewed — whether associated with success or failure — contain valuable lessons for other managers considering going international. The lessons should tilt the scales toward success when those other managers make their own firm international.

1.1 Going international

Going international is a series of independent stages in the geographical expansion of a firm. From a base in the country of origin, the steps in going international can be ranked in terms of increasing risk: exporting, agency representation overseas, overseas licensing, overseas sales subsidiary and overseas production subsidiary.

This book is predominantly concerned with the last, and most risky, step: the setting-up and running of an overseas production subsidiary. (However, there is one chapter on the second-most risky step — the establishment and running of an overseas sales subsidiary — since many of the problems are similar to those found with an overseas production subsidiary.)

The emphasis is upon the overseas production subsidiaries simply because of the risk. With any one of the other steps (even the overseas sales subsidiary), the amount of capital at risk is zero or small; in fact the step can usually be reversed with little or no loss. In the case of an overseas production subsidiary the position is quite different. Because production is involved, capital, often in considerable amounts, must be risked (in plant, equipment, etc.). Further, if the step is a mistake and a new decision to pull back is taken, all or substantial amounts of the capital might be lost. In fact, there are cases, quoted subsequently, where even the survival of the home-based operations was in doubt because of the problems with the overseas production subsidiary.

Thus, because of the difference in risk between it and the four other steps, this book concentrates upon only the one step in the process of going international, and examines in some detail the setting up and the subsequent running of forty-three overseas production subsidiaries as a basis for identifying the factors which promote success.

1.2 The interviews

The firms which were asked to participate in the study had consolidated sales in 1974-5 of £10 million or less, and had set up their first overseas production subsidiary in recent years.*

All firms fulfilling the criteria and willing to be interviewed were interviewed with the result that this report is based upon the experiences of forty-three smaller firms. The questionnaire, shown as Appendix III, was used and one or more directors of the firm were interviewed by at least two of the authors. The persons interviewed were most commonly those who had set up the firm's first overseas production subsidiary. In a few cases, the persons interviewed had not set up the subsidiary, but were now responsible in the UK for the subsidiary's performance.

The interviews, as can be seen from the subsequent chapters, or the questionnaire, stress the establishment and running of the *first* overseas production subsidiary. The reason is that in the first subsidiary the whole process is likely to be tackled much more simply, and clear mistakes and clear luck are more likely to be apparent than in subsequent ventures. From a methodological viewpoint, this simplification is likely to lead to a clearer observation of the links between decision and success.

The interviews then are directed toward determining the cause of success and failure in smaller firms setting up overseas production subsidiaries, by drawing upon the collected experiences of managers of smaller firms which in recent years set up overseas production subsidiaries for the first time.

1.3 Chapters 2 to 10

This section introduces the nine chapters which make up the body of this report. One chapter explains how the firms were selected for participation in the report, seven are concerned with the setting-up and the running of overseas production subsidiaries and one is concerned similarly with overseas sales subsidiaries.

---

*The comments are introductory only. See Chapter 2 for full details of the sampling scheme.

Chapter 2 describes how firms which had overseas subsidiaries were identified and how from these firms, forty-three were eventually interviewed. The chapter then proceeds to describe the industrial activity, the ownership and the size of these firms.

Chapter 3 starts the analyses of the experiences of the forty-three firms by examining the success of their overseas production subsidiaries. Success is defined in a variety of ways: profitability, the firms' own perceptions of success, the growth of the subsidiaries, the willingness to undertake subsequent overseas ventures, and the growth in exports from the UK firm. These factors are combined to give an overall success rating of 0 to 4 for each subsidiary. These success ratings are employed in every chapter to relate decisions to success, and accordingly Chapter 3 is an important chapter in the overall scheme. Apart from that main objective, the chapter also presents sketches of the firms which closed their overseas production subsidiaries and, to balance this, sketches of the six subsidiaries which were rated as '4', 'totally successful'.

Chapters 4 to 8 inclusive represent a series of consecutive stages in setting-up and subsequently running an overseas production subsidiary. While the chapters might represent a logical sequence of decisions, not all the overseas production subsidiaries were in practice established in this sequence; however the sequence has been maintained for all forty-three subsidiaries in order to deal efficiently with their experiences. Chapter 4 is concerned with the preliminary stages, Chapter 5 with planning, Chapter 6 with investing, Chapter 7 with controlling the subsidiary after it is in production and Chapter 8 gathers together the lessons learned and the problems encountered. These five chapters are the substance of this report and contain numerous indications of links between particular decisions and the level of success or failure.

Chapter 9 compresses into one chapter the five-chapter sequence for overseas production subsidiaries just described and examines the success, the establishment and the controlling of overseas sales subsidiaries.

Chapter 10 lists those features, analysed in the preceding chapters, which appear to characterise the successful overseas subsidiary.

Taken as a whole, the ten chapters should provide for those managers who are willing to be guided by other managers sufficient experiences to enable their own venture overseas to be more successful.

1.4 The appendices

The report is completed by three appendices. The first lists country-by-country the regulations, policies and inducements for inward investment. Appendix II is a brief summary of exchange control policy since permission from the exchange control authorities is needed for *all* outward investment from the UK (other than to the British Isles and Gibraltar). Appendix III reproduces for reference purposes the questionnaire used in the interview on which the report is based.

Executive summary

This chapter is introductory and indicates that the main emphasis in the book is upon the most risky step in going international: the setting-up and running of an overseas production subsidiary. Thus apart from one chapter on overseas sales subsidiaries, the chapters report upon the experiences of managers in forty-three firms in setting-up and running their first overseas production subsidiaries. The underlying aim is to provide a synthesis of these experiences for other managers to improve their own decisions on going international.

2 The firms in the sample

This chapter describes the method of selecting those firms whose experiences in setting up their first overseas production subsidiary constitute the data for this book. In addition, the chapter describes the industrial, ownership and size characteristics of the firms, and the size characteristics of the overseas production subsidiaries.

2.1 Method of selection

Official sources in foreign countries were asked to supply the names of firms in their country which were owned, wholly or in part, by a UK firm. Where possible, the name of the UK firm was also asked for. Lists were supplied by twelve of the fifteen countries approached.* Using UK official and trade sources the lists were then cross-checked and additions and amendments made. The lists at this stage showed 2259 UK firms. Each firm was then checked in respect of size and ownership. Firms were excluded for which consolidated sales

---

*Two countries, Canada and New Zealand, indicated that to their knowledge no such list exists, and another, Italy, indicated that the list is confidential.

in 1974-5 exceeded £10 million. Also firms were excluded which on checking further were found to be owned or controlled by firms of that size or larger. Of the original 2259 firms, 174 remained and these 174 are the basic sample for the research.

At this stage it was not known whether the overseas units of these 174 firms were sales or production subsidiaries, nor was it known which ones were 'first', rather than subsequent overseas ventures, or even the year of establishing the ventures. Accordingly, the managing directors of the 174 firms were contacted and asked:

1. 'Do you own a production unit abroad?'
2. 'When did the first production unit abroad commence operations?'
3. 'Are you or a fellow director willing to discuss your first overseas venture with us?'

Table 2.1 shows the break-down of the responses to this initial inquiry.

Table 2.1 Responses to initial enquiry

Response	Number of firms	%
An overseas production subsidiary established postwar and willing to be interviewed	43	25
No overseas production (but 30 interested in project and therefore received overseas sales subsidiary questionnaire)	64	37
Overseas production subsidiary established pre-1939	11	6
UK sales turnover 1974-75 in excess of £10 million	3	2
UK firm in hands of receiver	2	1
Official information wrong	3	2
Not interested	4	2
No response	44	25
	174	100

8   *Going International*

In Table 2.1 the two important entries are, first, the forty-three firms which had set up their first overseas production subsidiary in the postwar period and were willing to be interviewed, and second, the thirty firms which had established their first overseas *sales* subsidiary in this period.

In each of the forty-three firms at least one senior manager was interviewed face-to-face by at least two of the authors, using a structured and pre-tested set of questions. (The questions are reproduced in Appendix III.) For many of the forty-three firms the involvement extended beyond this formal interview. The experiences, as reported in the interviews, of the forty-three firms which had set up their first overseas production subsidiary in the postwar period constitute Chapters 3 to 8 inclusive.

In respect of the thirty firms which expressed interest in the project, but had not in fact set up an overseas production subsidiary, a postal questionnaire was devised about the problems of setting up a first overseas *sales* subsidiary and sent to these thirty firms. Nine questionnaires were returned and these are discussed in Chapter 9.

As these nine questionnaires were returned anonymously, the sample characteristics of the firms setting up their first overseas sales subsidiaries cannot be described. The remainder of this chapter therefore describes only the characteristics of those forty-three firms which had set up their first overseas production subsidiaries in the postwar period.

2.2 Industrial classification of firm

The forty-three firms were classified by their main industrial activity using the 1968 Standard Industrial Classification (SIC). The result, together with some supplementary information, is in Table 2.2.

Table 2.2 shows that the forty-three firms produced a wide variety of products and services. None of the overseas

Table 2.2 Standard Industrial Classification (SIC) of firm

SIC order	SIC description	Number of firms	Technology 'High'	'Low'	Year of establishing first overseas production subsidiary
IV	Coal and Petroleum Products	1	1	—	1962
V	Chemicals and Allied Industries	3	2	1	1962, 1967, 1970
VI	Metal Manufacture	3	2	1	1958, 1961, 1975
VII	Mechanical Engineering	8	6	2	1948, 1956, 1960, 1961, 1966, 1967, 1973, 1974
VIII	Instrument Engineering	3	3	—	1960, 1973, 1974
IX	Electrical Engineering	4	3	1	1959, 1963, 1973, 1973
XI	Vehicles	3	1	2	1960, 1960, 1964
XII	Metal Goods not elsewhere specified	10	4	6	1956, 1958, 1962, 1963, 1968, 1968, 1968, 1972, 1972, 1973
XIII	Textiles	2	—	2	1962, 1969
XIV	Leather, Leather Goods and Fur	1	—	1	1969
XV	Clothing and Footwear	2	—	2	1951, 1970
XVI	Bricks, Pottery, Glass, Cement, etc.	1	—	1	1951
XVIII	Paper, Printing and Publishing	1	—	1	1956
XIX	Other Manufacturing Industries	1	—	1	1961
		43	22	21	

production subsidiaries commenced with a product or service which was not already provided in the UK: consequently an industrial classification of overseas production subsidiaries by product is the same as for the UK. In seven cases UK firms' activities are spread over more than one standard industrial classification order, but the activities of the overseas production subsidiaries are confined to a main UK product division. The firms produced intermediate and component products and services (those for use by other firms in their own processes) and final products and services (those for actual final use). Of forty-three firms, thirty-six made producer goods or services, four consumer goods or services, and three were involved in both producer and consumer activities. For additional information, the forty-three firms have been divided into 'high technology' and 'low technology' on the basis of research expenditure. The sample splits as evenly as it can between high and low technology.

As supplementary information, Table 2.2 shows the year in which the first overseas production subsidiary was established. Both the average and the median age of the overseas production subsidiaries are eleven years. There appears to be no relationship between the industrial activity of the UK firm and the year in which the first overseas production subsidiary was set up.

In terms of industrial classification there appear to be no lessons for managers of firms contemplating going international. Since all the subsidiaries began life with a product or service already familiar to the UK parent firm, there is clearly no lesson since there is no comparison with a subsidiary which went ahead with a new product or service. Equally, the wide range of products or services and the lack of trend over time contain no lessons. Table 2.2 is therefore simply a description of the sample firms.

2.3 Ownership of firm

The ownership characteristics of the forty-three firms at the time of the establishment of the first overseas production subsidiary are shown in Table 2.3.

By the date of the interview, the ownership characteristics

Table 2.3 Ownership of firm

At the time of the first overseas production subsidiary

Private limited company	19
Public limited company	9
Quoted public limited company	15
	43

At the time of interview

Private limited company	16
Public limited company	7
Quoted public limited company	17
Subsidiary of larger organisation	3
	43

were slightly different: some were merely changes through time, such as a private limited company expanding its number of shareholders beyond fifty and thus becoming a public limited company, or obtaining a quotation for its shares; but in three cases the firms have become subsidiaries of other firms during the preparation of the survey. Since these acquisitions were so recent (in one case less than one week) and the men who had set up the overseas production subsidiaries were still in employment, the firms were left in the sample.

While the lesson is not clear, it is interesting to note that some firms indicated that the success of their foreign production subsidiaries had helped them toward quotation status, while others noted that the success of their overseas production subsidiaries had made them attractive to takeovers.

2.4 Size of firm

In respect of size, the upper limit for inclusion in the survey was set at £10 million consolidated turnover 1974-5, but below this ceiling the forty-three firms varied greatly.

Using sales as the measure of size, the spread is shown in the two left-hand columns of Table 2.4. The sample splits at £4 million. Twenty-two firms have sales of £4 million or less and twenty-one firms have sales of £4.1 million or more. An alternative measure of size is numbers employed, as shown in the two right-hand columns of Table 2.4. There is a fairly

Table 2.4 Size of firm

Sales 1974-75 £m.	Number of firms	Number of employees 1974-75	Number of firms
0-2	10	1-100	6
2.1-4	12	101-400	13
4.1-6	5	401-900	15
6.1-8	5	901-1500	5
8.1-10	11	1501-	4
	43		43

high correlation between the two halves of the table (that is, firms with high sales tend to employ more people) but there is some switching between the two halves indicating merely that sales per employee vary between firms.

Perhaps the main point to note in respect of Table 2.4 — and the only lesson for other firms — is the ability of small firms to 'go international'. Ten firms with sales of less than £2 million, six of which had less than one hundred employees, went international to the fullest extent of establishing a production unit overseas.

2.5 Size of overseas production subsidiary

To give an impression of the size of the overseas production subsidiaries, the sales for the subsidiaries were collected and these are shown in Table 2.5.

The sales of the UK parent were shown for 1974-5, which were the most recent figures when the research began. For the overseas production subsidiaries it has been decided to show the sales current at the time of interview (largely because these figures were accessible) and hence the appropriate date is 1976-7. The sales in 1976-7 obviously depend upon a range of factors. Four important ones are length of existence, initial

Table 2.5   Size of overseas production subsidiary

Sales 1976-77 £m.	Number of subsidiaries	Number of employees 1976-77	Number of subsidiaries
0-0.25	6 (2)	1-25	14 (4)
0.26-0.50	10 (2)	26-50	6 (2)
0.51-1.00	8 (2)	51-100	13 (3)
1.01-2.00	14 (4)	101-200	7 (2)
2.01-	5 (1)	201-	3
	43 (11)		43 (11)

(Numbers in parentheses refer to the peak figures of closed or sold subsidiaries — see page 14.)

scale of operations chosen, method of entry, and success. Age is important because recent ventures may not yet have attained full utilisation of capacity; initial scale of production may have been determined by the technological characteristics of production as much as by any other factor; and greenfield ventures start from a minimal base of sales turnover and employees in comparison with the acquisition form of entry. Not least, of course, some overseas production subsidiaries have been more successful than others and have expanded; consequently they are now well-established in foreign markets and no longer resemble the small units which were originally set up. These considerations are evaluated at length in the following chapters. The aim of this section is to give an overall impression of size.

Given this objective and despite the qualifications of comparison, the two left-hand columns of Table 2.5 show the current sales turnover of the first overseas production subsidiaries and the right-hand half gives the current employment totals. The first point that stands out is again the variation in size, but perhaps more important, it is obvious that some of the overseas production subsidiaries are surviving, even prospering, with turnover of less than £250 000 and many are surviving, even prospering, with less than twenty-five employees.

Firms who had closed or sold the overseas production subsidiary prior to the interview were asked the *peak* sales turnover and the *peak* employment attained by the subsidiary. These firms are noted in parentheses in the table.

On the basis of the data in the table, perhaps the most appropriate comment is again one of encouragement to other small firms, for its emerges that an overseas production subsidiary can be of quite modest size and can survive, or prosper, in overseas markets.

Executive summary

A short description of the basic characteristics of a sample is a prerequisite in any survey research, and this chapter has provided this description. That main objective apart, the main lesson for managers contemplating setting up an overseas production subsidiary is that the home-based firm can be quite small (sales of £2 million or less, one hundred employees or fewer), the overseas production subsidiary can be even smaller (sales £0.25 million or less, twenty-five employees or fewer) and the overseas production subsidiary can at least survive and in most cases prosper. Clearly size is no great barrier to going international.

3 The success of overseas production subsidiaries

The smaller firm differs from the large in the greater attention it has to pay to 'the bottom line'. The amount of profit — that which is left on the bottom of the profit and loss account after all expenses and claims have been met — is crucial to the smaller firm. The amount of profit is ultimately the source of survival to the smaller firm, and, in the shorter term, it determines too the friendliness of the bank manager, for the smaller firm has no muscle at the bank, nor in the corridors of government so increasingly and easily accessible to the large firm. The smaller firm therefore has to tread more carefully, for if a mistake is made it will have to rely on its own resources to recover. Additionally to the typical owner/manager, the bottom line is still a source of pride, an indication of a job well done, of competition met and beaten. For many smaller firms the success of the firm and of the man who runs it, is one and the same thing — the firm is the man. Hence most likely the most important question this book can answer is the simple one: *'Was the overseas production subsidiary successful?'*.

3.1 The range of success

Needless to say, not all the firms interviewed had met with

resounding success in their first manufacturing venture overseas. Indeed, had all met with resounding success, this book would have no value! The only possible advice would have been to invest abroad, anyhow and anywhere. Equally, not all met with total failure, so the simple but opposite advice is also wrong. Happily, the situation usual in most business activity also exists in connection with the first overseas production subsidiary of the firms in this sample: that there was a range of outcomes from wild success to catastrophic failure. In more than one case the overseas production subsidiary saved the firm from extinction and several firms had huge successes on their hands. At the other extreme, chairmen of two firms both used the phrase 'a complete disaster' to describe the first overseas production subsidiary, and the managing director of a third firm labelled the overseas venture as 'a joke'. In between lay a variety of situations of moderate success and failure, and it is probably in these, rather than the more extreme situations, that the real lessons for other firms lie.

The following sections identify the indicators or yardsticks of success and the chapter concludes by a summary, dividing the firms into groups according to the overall success of their first overseas production subsidiary.

3.2 Success: profitability

As profit is so important to the small firm, it was appropriate that profitability should form part of the discussion in the interviews. Accordingly the question was asked: 'In the *current* year, how does performance overseas compare with that in the UK in terms of profitability?'. Discussions then indicated that of the various measures of profitability, the rate of return on capital employed was perhaps the most appropriate for the firms in the sample. The forty-three responses are shown in Table 3.1.

Table 3.1

In the current year, how does performance overseas compare with with that in the UK in terms of profitability?

The overseas production subsidiary is more profitable than the UK operations	11
The overseas production subsidiary is equal in profitability to that of the UK operations	9
The overseas production subsidiary is less profitable than the UK operations	12
The overseas production subsidiary has been closed, or sold	11
	43

At the first glance at Table 3.1, perhaps the most striking feature is the eleven firms which could not answer the question because their overseas production subsidiaries have been closed or sold prior to the current year. More will be said about these shortly as they clearly have importance in any discussion of success, but confining discussion here to profitability of ongoing ventures, it can be seen that the overall position is finely balanced. In eleven cases, the overseas operation was more profitable than the home operation, in twelve cases the reverse was true, and in nine there was some rough equality in the profitability of home and overseas operations.

The question had to be asked with some care because of the possibility of affecting the profitability of either the home or the overseas venture by adjusting the prices at which any goods are transferred between the two operations, or by charging varying proportions of UK overheads (for example, product research and development) to the overseas operation. Clearly, if a semi-finished component was the subject of trade, either way, between the home and the overseas operation, the price at which the component was transferred could enhance the profit of one operation to the detriment of the other. Similarly alteration of the allocation of overhead expenses has the same effect of reallocating profits internationally. At this point it is sufficient to say that in Table 3.1 calculations of profitability have allowed for the effects of transfer pricing, which is discussed at some length in Section 7.5.

Another possible problem in Table 3.1 requires introduction. A possible bias could exist if the overseas production subsidiaries were relatively recent, and therefore not yet settled to a regular level of profitability, but again discussion with the directors of the firm indicated only one case where it was believed that this factor was relevant and that 'in the near future' the recently-established overseas production subsidiary would move from profitability equal to the UK operation to profitability greater than the home firm. Apart from discussions at the time of the interviews, subsequent analysis of Table 3.1 did not show any relationship between relative profitability and the age of the overseas production subsidiary. (See the appendix to this chapter.)

On balance, while for the small firm profitability is of extreme importance, the summary of Table 3.1 must be that only one quarter of the sample (eleven out of forty-three) achieved greater profitability overseas than in the UK, and less than half (eleven plus nine out of forty-three) achieved overseas profitability at least equal to that in the UK. Emphasis must be upon the eleven rather than on the twenty, because an overseas investment must be a higher risk venture than a home-based operation (because of the lower level of knowledge about the political, economic, legal and social environment of a foreign country and because of the difficulties of managing a venture from a distance of hundreds or even thousands of miles). And, normally in business one expects a higher level of profitability to compensate for the higher levels of risk to which investment monies are exposed.

Thus on the basis of this reasoning, only eleven of the forty-three firms appear to be successful in terms of profitability when measured against the risks, and another nine are able only to match the UK profitability (that is, there is no compensation for the extra risks of investing overseas). There remain twelve firms whose level of profitability of overseas operations cannot be judged as successful. Further, if to these twelve are added some of the eleven firms which had to close their overseas operations or decided to sell them, then at least one third, and approaching one half, of the firms interviewed had met with a lack of success in investing overseas, when judged by the level of profitability of operations. (It is not possible to add in all the eleven failure/closure firms since some of these were 'successful' at the time of sale, but were sold because of a change in policy, or in at least one case where the sale was recognised as a wrong decision.)

3.3 Success: the firms' own perceptions

While some people, like the authors, would put profitability-greater-than-the-UK as the prime criterion for success, it was repeatedly obvious that many of the managers being interviewed had multiple objectives for their overseas investment. These objectives ranged from being patriotic (extending British influence abroad) to the simple but unpatriotic desire to get some capital out of the UK, with a whole range of economic and non-economic motives between these two extremes. Accordingly, it seemed appropriate to ask: 'Has the *actual outcome* of your first overseas venture met the expectations *you* held for it?' This question sought to determine what objectives existed in addition to the narrow confines of 'the bottom line'.

As Table 3.2 shows, fifteen overseas ventures failed to meet the expectations that had been held for them, so again about one third of the overseas ventures could not be regarded as successful. Amongst the firms who stated that the overseas production subsidiaries had not come up to expectations, only two firms expected their overseas production subsidiaries to achieve desired performance at some time in the future.

However, the remaining two thirds of the sample did meet expectations and in six cases expectations were exceeded, usually by a considerable margin. In fifteen cases the

Table 3.2

Has the actual outcome of your first overseas production subsidiary met the expectations you held for it?

The first overseas production subsidiary exceeded expectations	6
The first overseas production subsidiary met expectations	15
The first overseas production subsidiary met expectations, but after a longer period of time than anticipated	7
The first overseas production subsidiary failed to meet expectations	15
	43

subsidiary simply met expectations and this group in fact includes one subsidiary which before the interview had been sold at a substantial profit.

To these fifteen another seven firms can be added, which might be described as giving a 'qualified yes' in reply to the question in Table 3.2. These seven were isolated in order to indicate to other managers the existence of the sizeable proportion of the sample in which expectations were met *but* after a longer period of time than had been anticipated. The seven responses here are representative of a recurrent point of discussion that, in an overseas venture a longer period of time must be allowed between a decision taken and that decision coming to fruition. This is partly a function of the problems of managing at a distance and partly a function of simply not knowing the accepted procedures and the short cuts in the overseas country.

For example, the general expectations held for an overseas production subsidiary in the capital goods industry in the USA were to give it six years to establish itself, but expectations were not realised for nine years, and in the ninth year profit was only $41. The managers of the firm believed that the three year delay in the expectations horizon was due to their incorrect approach to selling in the USA given the 'different culture, different priorities and different methods of business in the USA'. The initial selling approach was low key and consultative in nature — the US buyers took this as a sign of

Success of overseas production subsidiaries

lack of confidence of the salesman in his product. A switch to more aggressive selling worked. Thus, knowledge of business practices in the host country is essential, as is planning for the setting-up of the overseas production subsidiary. Thus a visit from head office in Birmingham to a branch factory in Walsall may take an hour, to visit a factory in Holland may take five hours and some pre-planning, while a visit to a factory in Australia will take thirty-six hours and quite a lot of preparation. Again, to install a new piece of machinery in Walsall which must be checked by the local factory inspector may not be difficult, since the procedure — and perhaps even the individual inspector — is known. To do a similar thing in, say, Italy, can be very frustrating because weeks or even months must be allowed. These two examples are perhaps stating the obvious to many experienced managers, but the interviews showed again and again that the most commonly repeated mistake in overseas ventures is to allow insufficient time for a decision to come to fruition.

The question relating to expectations called for a subjective response and was augmented by a later question which was more objective: 'In the actual outcome, how did the results of overseas production compare with your objectives?'. The responses are shown in Table 3.3.

Table 3.3

In the actual outcome, how did the results of overseas production compare with your objectives?

Overseas production exceeded targets	6
Overseas production met targets	21
Overseas production failed to meet targets	12
No targets were set for overseas production	4
	43

Six overseas production subsidiaries had clearly exceeded their targets, even in one case to 'beyond our wildest dreams', and, a further twenty-one had met the targets. Hence in terms of a specific measure of success, some two thirds (twenty-seven out of forty-three) of the firms interviewed had met with success in their first overseas production subsidiary.

However, no fewer than twelve firms failed to meet targets. In one case there was a single reason — the firm established a production subsidiary in Australia in the belief that a tariff was imminent which would have effectively excluded from the Australian market any firm without a production facility in Australia, and the tariff did not materialise leaving the market open to import competition. (It perhaps ought to be added that although this overseas production subsidiary is classed as a failure in Tables 3.2 and 3.3, the overall strategy of the parent firm was achieved. The objective of maintaining its Australian market share was met by selling the overseas production subsidiary and servicing the market by a licensing agreement backed by exports from the UK.) There are two cases in which failure to meet production targets was spectacular. One subsidiary achieved only one tenth of planned output and the other was the one described as a 'joke'.

Overall there is a high correlation between Table 3.2 (the subjective expectations) and Table 3.3 (the objective expectations). On these criteria the conclusion must be that some two thirds of these first ventures into manufacturing overseas were successful.

3.4 Growth

Growth is perhaps the most consistent objective of businesses

Table 3.4

Have you expanded your operations in ...... since your first foreign investment took place?

Operations have been expanded	34
Operations have not been expanded	7
Operations have only recently begun	2
	43

of all sizes. There appears inherent in managers of all types, from the entrepreneur to the corporate man, a belief in growth. Accordingly, growth has been adopted as another measure of success or failure of the first overseas production subsidiaries in this survey. Growth was broken down into two areas: the first is achieved growth, which of course would have a bias against recently established subsidiaries, and the second concerns plans for the expansion of the scale of production at the overseas plant.

The question was asked: 'Have you expanded your operations in . . . since your first foreign investment took place?'. The responses are in Table 3.4 and the predominant response (thirty-four out of forty-three) was that expansion *had* taken place, and in two other cases the operation was too recent for expansion to be a relevant concern. In only seven cases had expansion not taken place. These seven have not all been sold subsequently for, in fact, of the thirty-four cases in which operations had been expanded seven had been sold, leaving only four other sold subsidiaries among the seven which had had no expansion.

To augment the use of growth as an indicator of success, it was also asked: 'Have you any plans to expand the scale of operations in . . . ?'. Table 3.5 shows the responses to this question. About one third of the firms (fifteen out of forty-three) had plans to expand the scale of operations in their overseas production subsidiary. *A priori,* this is a high figure, but the fact that one third of the sample has plans for expansion at *one single point in time* is a clear indicator of the success of overseas operations. This is reinforced by the fact that discussion made it clear that by 'expansion' the concern

Table 3.5

Have you any plans to expand the scale of operations in . . . ?

There are plans for expansion	15
There are no plans for expansion	17
The overseas production subsidiary has been closed, or sold	11
	43

was not with general expansion (for example, of money value of sales) but with the expansion of the physical capacity for production. The other point of note (in Table 3.5) is that the two firms which said that the subsidiaries were too recently established to make a positive response in Table 3.4, are, in Table 3.5, included among those firms with plans to expand the capacity of the overseas plant.

Perhaps the most stringent criterion of success concerning growth would be where an overseas production subsidiary has expanded (as in Table 3.4) and there were *in addition* plans for expanding it further (as in Table 3.5). One third of the sample of firms (fourteen out of forty-three) can meet this double condition.

3.5 Subsequent overseas ventures

The establishment of further overseas ventures is an indication that the first production subsidiary abroad was successful. In the outcome this simple view was found insufficient, for some of the firms experiencing failure in their first venture did make another venture overseas. Consequently the view must be generalised that the establishment of the first overseas production subsidiary gave the firm sufficient confidence about investing overseas. In short, lessons have been learned, problems mastered and confidence gained.

The actual question was: 'Has your company made any other foreign investments since the time of the first production venture abroad? . . . If yes, in which country(ies) did those subsequent foreign investments take place? . . . Can you briefly describe those investments?'. Table 3.6 shows the outcome of this multiple question and shows in aggregate that twenty-four of the forty-three firms had made another investment overseas.

One firm had, subsequent to its first overseas production subsidiary in West Germany, opened three further production subsidiaries, one each in France, the USA and Canada. This firm incidentally, in respect of its first overseas production

Table 3.6

Has your company made any other foreign investments since the time of the first production venture abroad? If yes: *In which country(ies) did those subsequent foreign investments take place? Can you briefly describe those investments?*

Three further overseas production subsidiaries have been set up	1
Two further overseas production subsidiaries have been set up	9
One further overseas production subsidiary and two overseas sales subsidiaries have been set up	1
One further overseas production subsidiary and one overseas sales subsidiary have been set up	2
One further overseas production subsidiary has been set up	9
One overseas sales subsidiary has been set up	2
	24

subsidiary, is not one classified as 'exceeded expectations' in Table 3.2, nor 'exceeded targets' in Table 3.3. The first overseas production subsidiary was however much more profitable than the UK operation and is classified accordingly in Table 3.1 and it had been expanded and there were plans for its further expansion. On balance, this firm would be characterised better by one of 'solid success' rather than the 'wildest dreams' epithet. In addition to the considerable overseas commitment by this one firm, no fewer than nine others had set up two further overseas production subsidiaries and twelve others had set up one further overseas production subsidiary. Some detail on the setting-up of subsequent overseas sales subsidiaries is also shown in Table 3.6 and while these involve less of a capital commitment than an overseas production subsidiary, they do nevertheless indicate that the firms are willing to commit capital to overseas ventures. Several firms undertook overseas licensing subsequently, but although this may be a way of gaining a foothold in an overseas market, no commitment of capital is required and such ventures are much less risky than direct overseas investment. Consequently they have not been counted into Table 3.6.

In connection with the learning experiences inherent in the first overseas production subsidiary, it is important to note that of the eleven firms which had closed or sold their first overseas production subsidiary, no fewer than eight had opened at least one other overseas production subsidiary and four of these had opened two later overseas production subsidiaries. One of these firms manufactures small specialised machines for a variety of industries, but primarily the food industry. The company opened its first overseas production subsidiary in Australia in 1961, and while the overseas production subsidiary was not successful the firm has opened two subsequent overseas production units, one in the USA and, more recently, one in Mexico. Through the operation of their Australian plant, several lessons were learned by the firm, including the difficulties in having a minority holding in a joint venture and how to manage and enforce decisions at a considerable distance. Given their knowledge, when their chief salesman decided after a visit to the USA that he could create a market there, the company set up production there, and, again with some learning under their belt, the firm decided to set up another unit in Mexico. Both ventures are taking increasing shares of the local markets.

The criterion of success, whether the firm made investments abroad other than in its first overseas production subsidiary, is an important one because it establishes that the first overseas production subsidiaries in being succesful can lead to subsequent ventures, or that the first overseas production subsidiary is a mechanism for learning, problem solving and decision making in a new environment and that the firm used its first overseas production subsidiary in gaining these valuable experiences. In summary, on this criterion of success twenty-four of the forty-three first overseas production subsidiaries were successful.

3.6 Success: exports from the UK

It is possible that the establishment of an overseas production subsidiary will stimulate exports from the UK to the country in which the overseas production subsidiary is established. This possibility is based largely on the 'presence' principle. This principle suggests that the establishment of an overseas production subsidiary acts as a sign of faith and a gesture of goodwill to which residents respond, not only by being more willing to buy from the overseas production subsidiary than was previously the case from the UK plant, but are now more willing to buy products from the UK plant which are not made by the overseas production subsidiary. In our discussions, this 'presence' factor seemed to be strongest in West Germany. As the chief executive of a small company which supplied specialised machinery to a limited range of industries said: 'There is a general opinion that investment overseas means a loss of wealth to the UK; in our experience it is the reverse. We have obtained many more orders from Germany because of our operations being resident in Germany. The German subsidiary means work for the UK and our employees know it. If we had not had the German subsidiary, the UK plant would have had no work at times . . . We're hoping to get set up in the USA.'

Some care is needed in attempting to determine whether exports from the UK have been stimulated by opening an overseas production subsidiary because, for example, the overseas production subsidiary may in the first instance be substituting its own output for the exports of the home factory to that country. (The most obvious example is where the firm sets up an overseas production subsidiary in its major export market to meet demand by local production rather than by exports.) However, even where this direct substitution exists, the 'presence' principle may stimulate the export sales of the other products of the UK plant, or the nature of the exports may change from being exports of a final product (that is, a product ready for sale) to being exports of intermediate products (that is, components or semi-finished products which need additional work by the overseas subsidiary to render them ready for sale).

With these qualifications in mind, it was asked: 'Since production began in . . . have this company's exports to . . . increased, remained the same, or declined?'. Table 3.7 shows the responses. In twenty-four firms, UK exports had increased, thus indicating the existence of the 'presence' factor. The increases were of course a mixture of increases in exports of

Table 3.7

Since production began in . . . , have this company's exports to . . . increased, remained the same or declined?

UK exports to......have increased	24
UK exports to......have remained the same	8
UK exports to......have declined	9
No UK exports at any time to......	2
	43

other products and the substitution of intermediate products for final products in sufficient volume to make up for the lower per unit value of intermediate products compared with final products. In addition, another eight firms had maintained their value of UK exports to the country in which an overseas production subsidiary had been established. If one expects that the establishment of an overseas production subsidiary will lead to a decline in UK exports (because of the substitution of local production for UK production), it is significant that three quarters of the firms in the sample (thirty-two out of forty-three) have at least maintained the value of their exports from the UK to the host country.

In only nine cases have exports declined; eight of those tend to confirm the simple expectation that the overseas production subsidiary merely substitutes local for UK production, but in one case a sort of reverse 'presence' factor was at play, because the firm felt that the failure of their overseas production subsidiary had rebounded and caused a decline in exports from the UK to that country. In the remaining two cases the question on exports was not relevant because there had been and were no exports. (Of course, overall the group gained because the sales from the overseas production subsidiary were a net addition to sales.)

In terms of success measured by exports, it appears that there was a common experience of *increased* exports after the establishment of the overseas production subsidiary, and it is in no way a criticism of the firms involved to say that to many of them the increase in exports was a surprise because they were unaware of, or had underestimated the importance of the 'presence' principle, or had underestimated the volume of components and intermediate products the overseas production subsidiary would demand from the UK production facilities.

3.7 Closures and sales

So far several criteria of success have been analysed individually and before summarising and coalescing these to gain a feel for the overall level of success in the establishment of forty-three overseas production subsidiaries, it is necessary to comment upon those eleven of the forty-three which were closed or sold before the date of the interviews.

Table 3.8 gives the basic data on the eleven overseas production subsidiaries. In four cases (the first four listed in Table 3.8) there was an actual capital loss incurred and the ventures can only be described as failures. In two cases the loss was of sufficient size to jeopardise the existence of the UK firm; these were the French venture 1970-74 and the Italian venture 1970-75. In the fifth listing (West Germany 1957-) the fate of the overseas production subsidiary is still in the balance, and in the remaining six cases the overseas production subsidiaries were sold at a capital profit — in the final case, the present management clearly recognised that the decision to sell was a straight mistake, but at the time (1964) sale was considered to be the best policy.

Each of the eleven ventures will now be summarised to

Table 3.8 Closures and sales of overseas subsidiaries before the date of interview

Country and period of operation		Notes
France	1970-74	Closed — all capital lost, UK firm threatened.
Italy	1970-75	Given away to Italian partner — all capital lost, UK firm threatened.
France	1960-72	Closed — all capital lost.
South Africa	1961-68	Sold to a UK competitor apart from some debts; profit remitted exceeded capital investment — on balance some capital lost.
West Germany	1957-	Closed temporarily in 1974 due to recession, may be re-opened.
Belgium	1969-74	Closed — royalties and remittances exceeded capital investment sum but losses made because of debt interest.
Belgium	1973-75	Sold — no capital lost.
Australia	1956-73	Sold — no capital lost.
Australia	1961-73	Sold — no capital lost.
Belgium	1960-74	Sold — no capital lost.
USA	1956-64	Sold — for twice capital investment ('sale a mistake').

indicate the dominant cause of the closure or sale. These cases, as well as the successes, will also be referred to in subsequent chapters.

In the case of the venture into France in 1970 (which was closed in 1974), a French nobleman approached the UK firm 'out of the blue' with a proposal to manufacture in France on some land owned by a friend. The firm admits now that they were 'led on' by 'the Count' and they did not explore the market themselves and in fact once the plant was established they were quite unable to compete with the local producers on price, which appeared to be more important in France than quality, and quality was the firm's selling strategy in the UK. The firm noted: 'We wish to take part in your survey to pass on our experience to other small firms since we nearly did not survive our first overseas production venture'.

Another huge failure was the venture into Italy, conceived in 1970; the first production began in September 1973 and the

Success of overseas production subsidiaries 31

UK firm pulled out in mid-1975 in order to prevent the UK firm from going under. A synthesis of the failure in this case would be that a major part of the problem was in attempting to develop an automated plant, whereas the UK plant was labour intensive, so that the UK experience of production, even though the product was identical, was not directly useful and the problems that occurred in setting up a new method of production were magnified greatly by distance. Perhaps the plant could have been put up successfully had the country not been Italy. As the country was Italy, the problems were compounded by recurrent strikes (among suppliers, contractors, postal workers) and the different standards of bookkeeping, business and workmanship that exist in Italy when compared with much of the remainder of Europe. Apart from the delays in building the plant, which were costly, the highest level of production achieved was ten per cent of that for which the plant was designed.

In order to minimise communication problems, the third firm in Table 3.8 opened its first overseas production subsidiary in France and in fact it was quicker to go from the head office and major plant site in the UK to the French plant than to the other UK plant. However a recurrent problem was that customs and business methods were different in France and the UK and, in particular, the firm did not make enough effort to integrate into the French scene. As the managing director noted: 'We were a British company operating in France'. The firm had a Briton (although fluent in French) as a chief executive, who in the firm's later view did not pay sufficient attention to the local dignitaries and in particular the mayor, and had an advertising policy that was insufficiently French. These were all identified by the firm in the interview as relevant to the failure. In addition the firm noted (as in the other French failure above) that they found in France a price differential of ten to fifteen per cent would not be paid for the higher quality product.

The South African failure relates to an overseas production subsidiary begun in 1961. A local manufacturing firm was purchased after the importer had pointed out the opportunity. A senior executive, currently on holiday in Kenya, flew to South Africa and concluded the deal. Initially all went well until the death of a key man in 1965, after which problems occurred under the new manager — the former auditor of the firm — and the situation went from bad to worse. The interview established clearly therefore the choice of the post-1965 manager as the sole cause of failure.

At this point in progressing through Table 3.8 it is perhaps no longer appropriate to talk of failure; for the remaining cases closure or sale did occur but not necessarily because of failure. In no case from this point onwards was the closure or sale to involve the firm in losses. In fact in some cases, a considerable gain was made. While incompetence may have been the cause in the South African case, in he case of the West German operation, 1957—   , the cause was believed to be dishonesty. A West German was in charge and a misappropriation of £90 000 was apparent, with the possibility of the sum being larger, though an international firm of accountants failed to establish the means of misappropriation. This cash drain caused difficulties and together with the recession in that trade in Germany, the plant was closed in 1974, though it may be reopened when the next boom is well under way and local producers are running short of capacity.

Another failure in Table 3.8 was a Belgian overseas production subsidiary begun in 1969 and closed down in 1974. The firm was approached at a trade fair by a Belgian firm which was in difficulties and needed a partner. The major cause of failure of the overseas production subsidiary was precisely that already affecting the Belgian firm: the market, which was fashion-based, was changing, leaving excess capacity in its wake. The firm noted that they had not thought of investing overseas until approached at the trade fair.

Belgium is also the scene of the next venture in this brief summary of Table 3.8. The overseas production subsidiary was established in 1973 and was sold in 1975. The experience was brief but forceful. The firm was led to set up the subsidiary by an American multinational (an existing customer) which said it could give them more work if they had an outlet in Belgium. The outlet was opened but the US firm failed to supply the orders, and the sole problem became one of finding sales; in less than three years three chief executives were tried to get the sales volume to sustain the plant. They all failed and the plant was sold.

Sales were present in Australia for the eighth firm listed in Table 3.8, and in fact the firm had been exporting there since before World War II. The production operation was set up in 1956 by the then sales manager, who became the chief executive of the Australian subsidiary. In the firm's view this appointment was the cause of the failure because 'he became more Australian than the Australians', a derogatory remark which when clarified, proved to mean that he was excessively independent and loath to take instructions from head office. The firm, with hindsight, felt that a local (Australian) manager would in the event have proved less independent. It also found impossible at a distance of twelve thousand miles to gain a feel for, much less have control over, the subsidiary and eventually they decided to sell (in 1973) as by then it was quite obvious that sales had not kept in line with the growth of the Australian economy or their competitors.

The ninth firm listed in Table 3.8 has already been substantially covered. It began production in Australia in 1961 in anticipation of a tariff barrier by Australia which would close the Australian market on the firm's sales from the UK, and the tariff failed to materialise. However in the twelve years of operation the firm felt it had 'no control over what the Australian subsidiary made or did' — again a reflection of the very real problems imposed by twelve thousand miles of separation.

Returning to Belgium for the penultimate firm in Table 3.8, the overseas production subsidiary was set up in 1960 in order to speed up deliveries to the (new) EEC market, and hopefully to cut costs by avoiding the transport charges reckoned to be at that time about twenty per cent on top of the

UK ex-works cost. The overseas production subsidiary was a joint venture and the Belgians had responsibility for production while the Britons had responsibility for sales. Needless to say (with the benefit of hindsight) any problem was blamed by the one on to the other, and there were in the early years considerable nationalistic tendencies against UK operations in the EEC. The running fights between the two sides in the joint venture coupled with the fact — increasingly obvious — that the real market for the product lay in West Germany rather than Belgium or the EEC, led the UK firm to sell its share in 1974 and concentrate on export selling.

In the final case in Table 3.8 it is totally inappropriate to talk of failure. The subsidiary in the USA was a success. It was established in 1956 and in 1959 had a sales value of £1.5 million on which the net profit was £0.5 million. The respondent in the interview believed something unknown to him (he was a less senior manager at the time) must have happened to prompt the sale, but the figures showed it to be a continuously profitable operation and ought never to have been sold.

It is perhaps curious that Table 3.8, showing those overseas production subsidiaries closed or sold before the date of the survey interview, contains the full spectrum of success and failure, from those ventures which threatened the existence of the UK firm to one which was extremely profitable. Accordingly, Table 3.8 cannot be viewed as a list of failures, but only as a list of those overseas production subsidiaries which for one reason or another had been closed or sold.

3.8 The overall level of success

Success is not uniquely measurable in business; accordingly Sections 3.2 to 3.6 indicated five criteria which might appear to be important to the average person. The five are: profitability (to which some would lend most weight); the firm's own perceptions of 'success' — both subjective and objective; growth, both achieved and planned; the willingness to invest in later overseas ventures; and the behaviour of exports following the establishment of the overseas production subsidiary.

Accepting profitability as important to the smaller firm, Table 3.1 showing 'comparative profitability in the UK and overseas', was taken as the standard and the starting point. It was adjusted on the basis of results on the other four criteria for success. In effect this amounted to a simple group ranking procedure so that at the end of the process there were six firms which could be labelled 'totally successful' since they appeared in the highest category of success on *each* of the five criteria; similarly the label 'very successful' would indicate the firms (in fact nine in number) which were in the highest grade on all but one criterion.

This process was continued to give the labels shown in Table 3.9, and for subsequent use a 'rating' as well as a label has been given to each category. Figure 3.1 puts the results in Table 3.9 into a simple display form. Using 'average success' or 'rating 2' as the standard level of success that the average firm might expect, it can be seen that the distribution of success is slightly skewed toward success rather than failure in that fifteen (nine plus six) firms have experienced success greater than average, and thirteen (eight plus five) have experienced success less than average. Of those with a comparative lack of success, the firms listed in Table 3.9 which at the date of interview

Table 3.9 The overall level of success of the first overseas production subsidiary

Label	Rating	Number of firms/subsidiaries
Totally successful	4	6
Very successful	3	9
Average success	2	15
Not successful	1	8
Failure	0	5
		43

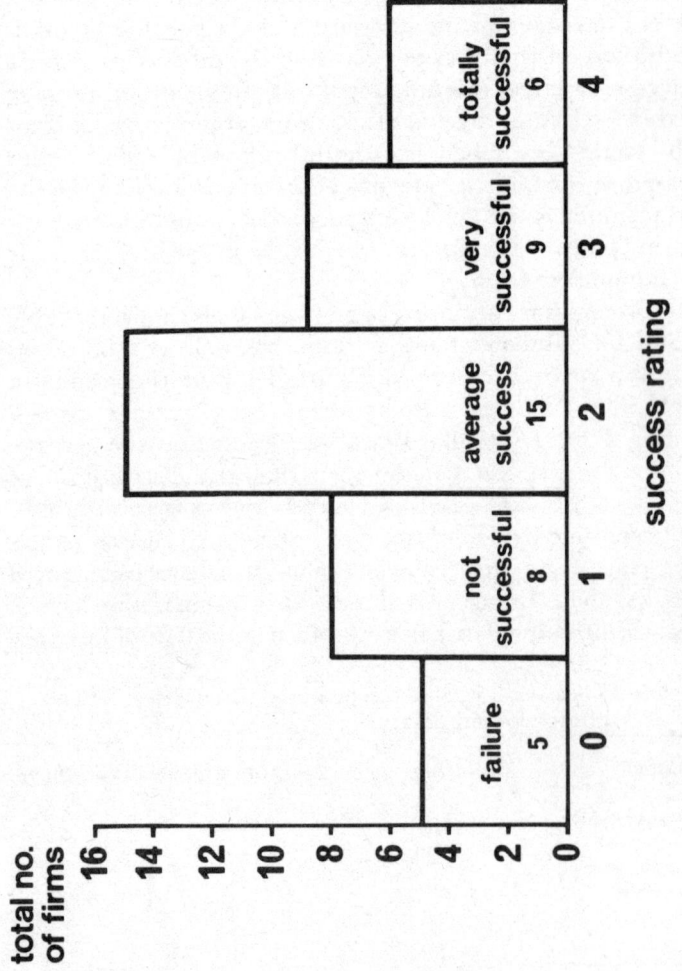

Figure 3.1 The overall level of success of the first overseas production subsidiary

had been closed down or sold can be found in the '1' and the '0' ratings with two exceptions (USA 1956-64, '2', Belgium 1960-74, '2'). The mean success rating of all firms is 2.1.

This short section is important since in all subsequent tables, the rating given in this section will be used to rank the methods and decisions used in going international. By judging the outcomes of decisions by the associated success ratings, prescriptive or pretentious comments on 'how things should have been done' are avoided and an increase in objectivity is achieved.

3.9 Totally successful ventures

Because some space was spent in Section 3.7 commenting on the closures and sales, it is appropriate to conclude this

Table 3.10 The 'totally successful' overseas production subsidiaries

Country and date of establishing overseas production subsidiary	Investor's comments
Luxembourg, 1958	'Invested £2500, subsequent loans have been repaid in full. Non-financial assistance which has a tangible value was made available. Current turnover is £5 million p.a.'
West Germany, 1959	'Invested £10 000, current sales are DM1.3 million, gross profit seventy-five per cent on sales.'
South Africa, 1964	'Initial problems until changed management, now thirty per cent return on assets.'
South Africa, 1968	'Profitability two-and-a-half times that of the UK operation.'
Netherlands, 1969	'In first two years, sales double those expected.'
West Germany, 1973	'Exports in 1972 were £200 000, now turnover is £1.25 million, ten per cent net return on sales, thirty per cent on total assets.'

chapter with a brief commet on the six firms which on the basis of the criteria could be described as 'totally successful' (rating '4'). There is a brief listing in Table 3.10.

Taken chronologically, the first firm, perhaps the most successful of all, opened up its production subsidiary in 1958 in Luxembourg. The scale of the initial operation can be judged by the investment — £2500 — and it has been self-financing since and currently supports a turnover of £5 million. The first manager is still the chief executive and to him must go considerable credit, but a secondary factor in the success is that the product, in the leisure market, hit the growth in EEC standards of living just at the right time. In addition, the firm feels that its Luxembourg base offers an advantage in that there is nationalistic jealousy among the big economic powers in the EEC with the associated tendency to buy German, buy French or whatever, and Luxembourg poses no threat in this economic rivalry.

In the next year, 1959, another small UK firm invested £10 000 in West Germany and, as in the above case, began production, in rented premises, of exactly the same products as were produced in the UK and exported. Neither of these two firms took risks in new products, new methods of production, or the purchase of premises, until well established. Sales in the first year were DM23 000, in 1974-5 DM 306 000, and on the basis of its German experience the firm has production units in France, the USA and Canada. The German operation now has its own land and factory purchased out of profits. Overall it was described as 'a very smooth operation, which started off making good profits and never looked back'. Again without detracting in any way from the obvious managerial capabilities of all concerned, it is clear that a number of factors — management, market and production — must have coalesced to produce success of this magnitude.

The third firm shown in Table 3.10 did not have a smooth start and in fact small losses and small profits were shown for the first six years, (1964 to 1970), when the investment was changed from a forty per cent holding into a one hundred per cent owned subsidiary enabling changes based on UK experience to be put quickly into effect. This was combined with a change in top management of the subsidiary from South Africans to Britons, the latter being given whatever support staff was necessary from the UK. From this point the subsidiary grew and became extremely profitable, without any change in the design or production of the product.

South Africa is also the location of the fourth of the six 'total successes'. However, from its establishment in 1968 the subsidiary had no problems 'except the normal ones of running a business'; the firm has held eighty-two per cent of the equity from the start and has had no problems with its minority partners. The subsidiary produces only three standard products and, as noted in the table, profitability is two-and-a-half times that of the UK.

In 1969 the fifth 'total success' in the sample was established in the Netherlands. The amount invested was larger than in the previous four cases because the firm bought one hundred per cent of an existing (Dutch) manufacturer, rather than setting up a new venture as in the above cases. Within two years the sales of the venture were more than double those at the time of the takeover and the subsidiary is now eighty per cent of the size of the UK operation. No problems have occurred and the firm believes its success is due to continuing in Holland its UK policy of having professionally trained management — and more importantly in their view — sustaining a close relationship among persons at all levels of employment. In fact the Dutch firm was selected not because of its product or location, but because the firm felt the people in the firm at all levels would respond to this philosophy. But again without detracting from the abilities of the people involved, the success is such that the product and the market must also have matched.

The final 'totally successful' overseas production subsidiary in the sample began in 1973 in West Germany. In 1970 the firm bought an agency sales office in Cologne for £20 000 and lost £68 000 in the first year because the capacity of the sales office was greater than the sales achieved. The British chief executive (taken over with the office) was quickly replaced by a German who transferred the operation to Frankfurt and persuaded the UK firm to begin production there of three of its simpler products. (The major seller as it turned out later was a product that was not then exported to West Germany but the local man thought he would create a market for it if it was manufactured in Germany.) In 1972 exports though the sales office were £200 000 and in 1975 turnover of the factory was £1 250 000 giving a ten per cent net return on sales.

No attempt has been made in this section to relate success to cause, the subsequent chapters will do this in detail. This short section is present to give to other managers the flavour of the six successful operations. In six short paragraphs it is difficult to convey the level of success being delivered by these six overseas production subsidiaries. To an extent the figures can speak for themselves, but what the paragraphs fail to get across is the pleasure or exuberance, so obvious in the interviews, that resulted from successfully going international.

Executive summary

This chapter laid down five criteria of success for the smaller firm in setting up an overseas production subsidiary. On the basis of these five criteria the forty-three subsidiaries have been classified according to the level of success and failure. The classification is in Table 3.9 and it will be the basis for subsequent chapters which attempt to relate success (or failure) to specific actions and decisions. The classification has the additional benefit of avoiding prescriptive comments from the authors on 'how things should have been done' — thus, the methodology is to judge the outcomes of the actions and decisions by the objective standard of achieved success.

Appendix to Chapter 3

Chapter 3 has classified the forty-three firms in terms of achieved performance. Subsequent chapters will relate each firm's actions and decisions to its achieved performance. It is possible, however, that the success ratings are determined by a factor beyond the firm's control and hence any findings in subsequent chapters would be chance occurrences. It has been suggested for example that the date of establishment is one such factor — with the longer-established firms being the more successful on the ratings in Chapter 3; another suggested factor is the technology-intensity of the firm — with the high technology firms being the more successful; and a third factor is said to be the size of the parent firm — with the larger firms, having more resources and more professional managers, being the more successful.

These are possibilities that need to be proven or disproven before the book resumes its intended course. This appendix summarises analyses that show there is no correlation between any of the factors and the success ratings compiled in Chapter 3.

Tables A3.1, A3.2 and A3.3 summarise attempts to create a pattern between the success ratings and, respectively, the date of establishment, technology-intensity and the size of the parent firm. As the tables summarise, patterns could not be produced and the conclusion is that the suggested relationships do not exist. It is likely therefore that patterns found in subsequent chapters are not the result of underlying influences due to date of establishment, technology-intensity and the size of the parent firm, but are the result of specific managerial decisions.

Table A3.1 Date of establishment and success rating

Time of establishment of overseas production subsidiary	Number of firms	Mean success rating
1948-55	3	2.3
1956-60	10	2.1
1961-65	11	2.1
1966-70	9	2.1
1971-75	10	1.9
	43	

Table A3.2 Technology-intensity and success

	Number of firms	Mean success rating
High technology firms	22	2.0
Low technology firms	21	2.1
	43	

Table A3.3 Size of parent firm and success rating of overseas production subsidiary

Sales turnover of parent firm	Number of firms	Mean success rating
Less than £2.0 million	10	1.9
£2.1 million to £4 million	12	1.9
£4.1 million to £6 million	5	2.4
£6.1 million to £8 million	5	2.4
£8.1 million to £10 million	11	2.1
	43	

4 The preliminary stages

The previous chapter laid down criteria by which overseas production subsidiaries might be judged. Using these criteria for the forty-three overseas production subsidiaries in the sample, the criteria gave an overall success rating for each of the subsidiaries. (See summary in Table 3.9, page 35.) This chapter and the subsequent four chapters will match these success ratings against the particular decisions and actions taken in connection with each of the overseas production subsidiaries. For example, is success related to the route which led to the setting up of an overseas production subsidiary? Does it matter that some firms went straight from exporting to overseas production while others followed the more cautious route of exporting, appointing an agent and setting up an overseas sales subsidiary before taking the plunge into overseas production? These pre-investment factors and the levels of success are the concern of this chapter, and the subsequent chapters concentrate upon success related to the planning stages of the investment, to the investment itself, to the operational controls on the project once in operation, and to the problems found and lessons learned.

The experienced manager knows there is no business equivalent of the Holy Grail, and will appreciate that these chapters are not a fruitless search for it. What the chapters will attempt to show, however, is that on balance success goes to the deserving, and failure is typically the price of carelessness and folly. Business is no different to any other aspect of life and while some undeserving fool might scoop the jackpot occasionally, in general the higher levels of success have to be earned, and in business this is by means of good management.

4.1 The route to an overseas production subsidiary

As suggested above, there are several routes that lead to the establishment of an overseas production subsidiary. The most usual ones are:

A. From existing UK operations, direct to establishing an overseas production subsidiary — the 'direct' route.

B. From existing UK operations, to exporting to a country, to establishing an overseas production subsidiary there.

C. From existing UK operations, to exporting to a country, to appointing a foreign agent there, to establishing an overseas production subsidiary there.

D. From existing UK operations, to exporting to a country, to setting up an overseas sales subsidiary there, to establishing an overseas production subsidiary there.

E. From existing UK operations, to exporting to a country, to appointing a foreign agent there, to setting up an overseas sales subsidiary there, to establishing an overseas production subsidiary there — the 'full' route.

Figure 4.1 shows these five routes in diagramatic form; the essential difference between the five routes, highlighted by

Figure 4.1 Routes to investment in overseas production facilities

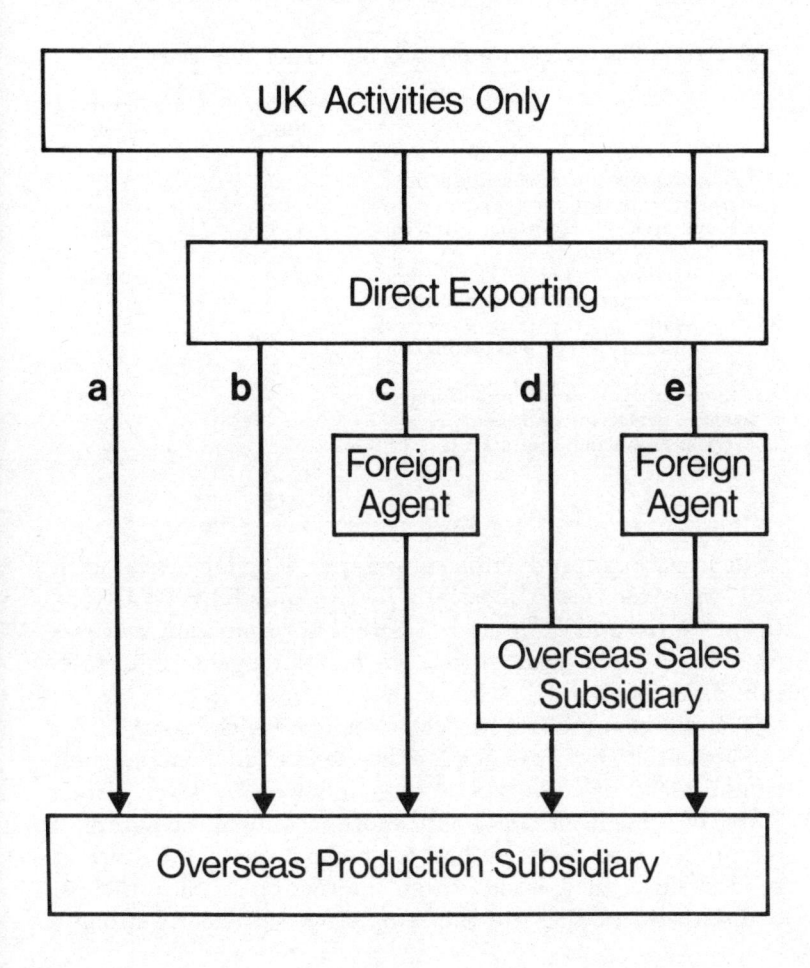

Figure 4.1, is that there are extra steps in the process between the 'direct' route and the 'full' route. The significance is that each step gives an opportunity for consolidating the experiences and the lessons learned, for assessing the value of decisions taken thus far along the route, and for making an informed judgement about the viability of the next step.

Using the five routes indicated, Table 4.1 shows the number of firms in the survey taking each route and the success ratings

Table 4.1 The route to the overseas production subsidiary

Route	Number of firms	Mean success rating
A. UK operations — overseas production subsidiary (the 'direct' route)	7	1.1
B. UK operations — exporting — overseas production subsidiary	9	1.9
C. UK operations — exporting — foreign agent — overseas production subsidiary	20	2.2
D. UK operations — exporting — overseas sales subsidiary — overseas production subsidiary	2	2.5
E. UK operations — exporting — foreign agent — overses sales subsidiary — overseas production subsidiary (the 'full' route)	5	2.8
	43	

of their overseas production subsidiaries. The factors for each firm were determined basically by two questions: 'Was your firm exporting to . . .?' and 'Before that production unit was established, had your firm ever had an agent or a sales subsidiary in . . .?'.

The direct route (Route A) — the one which has the least opportunities for learning, reassessment and incremental commitment of resources — was followed by seven firms. Three of these firms could not export because of the nature of the product and therefore had to plunge directly into overseas production if they wished to go international. Nevertheless, one sixth of the firms in the sample felt sufficiently strongly

The preliminary stages

about the viability of an overseas production subsidiary to go straight into production without prior experience of trading with or in the country, either through choice or necessity. The levels of success achieved by these subsidiaries were '2', '1', and '0' ('average success', 'not successful', 'failure') and the mean success rating for this group is 1.1.

The next possible route is one which allows the firm to learn about the country in which they are to site their first overseas production subsidiary by exporting to that country (Route B). The knowledge that can be learned by exporting is limited but *a priori* offers more learning than the 'direct' route. Nine firms followed this route and the full range of success and failure is found among the nine. However, the ratings were typically toward the lower scores and the average for the nine is 1.9.

Route C was followed by twenty firms, and is clearly the most popular. This route involves exporting and subsequently the use of an agent in the country as the two intermediate steps between UK-only activity and an overseas production subsidiary in that country. Again the full range of success can be observed and the overall mean for firms following this route is 2.2.

An alternative to an agent is an overseas sales subsidiary and two firms chose this route (Route D). They achieved 'very successful' and 'average success' ratings, with the result that the mean rating is 2.5.

Route E can be termed the 'full' route, which involves exporting, the use of an agent and the establishment of an overseas sales subsidiary prior to setting up an overseas production subsidiary and was followed by five firms. Two of these were 'totally successful' and though the other three achieved lower ratings, there were no 'failures' in this group. Overall this gave a mean rating of 2.8.

While it cannot be suggested that any statistical significance can be placed on the differences in the mean ratings for each route (because the sample of firms is too small to support refined statistical conclusions) it is interesting to observe that there is a monotonic pattern in the mean success ratings. The mean rating increases as more steps are included in the route to setting up an overseas production subsidiary. The table does suggest, as commonsense would, that on average success is higher for those firms that have taken a step-by-step approach to investing in an overseas production subsidiary. It appears that lessons can be learned from exporting, and from use of an agent, and from operating an overseas sales subsidiary, and that such lessons of past experience can be incorporated into decisions so that the chances of success for the overseas production subsidiary are improved.

Perhaps the impact of Table 4.1 can be strengthened by breaking down the 'popular' route (UK operations — exporting — foreign agent — overseas production subsidiary) followed by twenty firms into those whose sales to that foreign country were a material part of the total sales for the firm and those whose sales to that foreign country were a small part of the total. Early in the interviews, on the occasions when some reluctance to reveal figures was found, the level of five per cent of UK sales was mentioned to test the size of overseas sales (through exporting, a foreign agent and an overseas sales subsidiary). Adopting this level of five per cent of sales to the foreign country as the break between material and non-material proportion of total sales, the firms in Route C in Table 4.1 have been reclassified as shown in Table 4.2.

The split of the firms as shown in Table 4.2 is remarkable. Seven firms had a sales level of less than five per cent to the country and their success ratings give an overall success rating of 1.1. This success rating, for firms whose route to the establishment of an overseas production subsidiary was via exporting and a foreign agent but whose sales to the country were less than five per cent of total sales, is equal to that for the companies whose route was the direct one. Again, while this may be a commonsense conclusion, it does confirm the existence of successful learning in the process of going international.

There is further consistency in the findings. The remaining firms in Table 4.2, those thirteen firms who were exporting

Table 4.2 Route C in Table 4.1

	Number of firms	Mean success rating
Firms whose sales to the foreign country prior to the setting up of the overseas production subsidiary were *less* than five per cent of total sales	7	1.1
Firms whose sales to the foreign country prior to the setting up of the overseas production subsidiary were *greater* than five per cent of total sales	13	2.9
	20	

Scenario 4.1.1 Success rating: '1'

A Midlands firm supplying engineered parts to a whole range of consumer and capital goods customers set up its first overseas production subsidiary in Holland in 1973. They had not exported to Holland (therefore had not had an agent or an overseas sales subsidiary there either), but had concentrated for some time on breaking into the West German market. 'We had attempted exporting to West Germany, which has the biggest on-going and most viable industry — we wanted to get established in West Germany. We spent a lot of time in Germany and had tried three agents, and tried to form an association with a German firm similar to our own.' Then in 1973, through their auditors the firm heard of a firm in Holland willing to be taken over. The firm was taken over in 1973 and in 1975 recession hit Holland; the recession, together with the fact that the existing (Dutch) managing director was anti-German, meant the German market was still untouched.

more than five per cent of their production to the foreign country in which they were subsequently to establish a production subsidiary, have an average success rating of 2.9 — similar to those firms in Table 4.1 which followed the full route to the establishment of an overseas production subsidiary. This suggests again that where learning is in some sense obligatory (because recurrent contact with the country cannot do other than cause learning to take place) the level of success is increased dramatically.

This section has looked at the route to the establishment of an overseas production subsidiary. There are five routes typically followed ranging from the immediate launch of an overseas production subsidiary on the basis of UK experience to a step-by-step involvement with foreign markets. The findings in this section are consistent and suggest strongly that there is a connection between the route to an overseas production subsidiary and the level of success. Success, on average, goes to those firms which follow the longer routes to setting up an overseas production subsidiary because of the knowledge gained at each step on the route and the assessment

---

Scenario 4.1.2 Success rating: '3'

A firm with two distinct product groups, but both for heavy capital goods industries, first exported to South Africa in 1955, and in 1956 appointed an agent there. Exports grew to be a substantial proportion of production with the result that in 1965 an overseas sales subsidiary was set up in partnership with the agent, and in 1967 a decision was taken to go into production in South Africa due to the ever-advancing policy in South Africa of local manufacture enforced by tariff barriers. The overseas production subsidiary moved into profitability in 1969 and has stayed there, making a pre-tax return of twenty per cent on assets.

that is possible at each step before further resources are committed to that market. Equally, the lower levels of success and failure itself, on average, go to those firms which take the shorter routes and omit the opportunities for learning and reassessment. And, within the routes, it is likely that as with 'Route C' shown in Table 4.2, the higher the level of existing activity in the market prior to the setting up of the overseas production subsidiary, the more likely is the overseas production subsidiary to be successful. In short, the experiences of forty-three firms in setting up their first overseas production subsidiaries clearly suggest that proceeding step-by-step, and building up business at each step as a prelude to the next step, is the route to success in going international.

4.2 The impact of an outside stimulus

Whatever route actually led to the establishment of an overseas production subsidiary, there must have been some point at which the final step became a definite possibility. Perhaps the easiest of such points to identify is when the final step was prompted by an event or a person outside of the firm. In fact, seventeen firms of the forty-three in the survey had set up the overseas production subsidiary in response to an outside stimulus of this sort.

The question used in the interviews was 'What was the *single most important* factor that led your firm to make its first foreign investment in production facilities?'. When the factor was an outside event or person, the response to this question was usually quick. In other cases the decision point was more difficult to establish but for the seventeen firms which had reacted to an outside event or person, the summary is given in Table 4.3.

The seventeen firms can be divided into two responses: the seven which reacted to an approach by a person and the ten

Table 4.3

What was the single most important factor that led your firm to make its first foreign investment in production facilities?

Of the seventeen firms reacting to an outside stimulus:

Response	Number of firms	Mean success rating
'We were approached by . . . (a person)'	7	1.6
'A tariff (or similar) was expected'	10	1.9
Remaining firms	26	2.3
	43	

which reacted to the actual or threatened imposition of some kind of trade barrier by the host country.

For the seven firms for which the outside stimulus was some kind of personal approach to the firm, the average success rating, shown in Table 4.3, is 1.6. The full range of success is found but among the seven are two rated 'not successful' and two rated 'failure', thus lowering the average success rating for the group. The type of approach made to the firm varied. In Chapter 3, the approach by the French nobleman was mentioned, but this was not typical and the approach did result in a 'disaster' — to use the interviewee's description — and the overseas production subsidiary threatened the existence of the UK firm.

The other — perhaps more conventional — approaches were by the agent already handling his country's imports from the UK (two cases), a supplier to the UK firm who wanted to invest abroad and needed the firm's experience of the final product (one case), a customer of the UK firm in the country (one case), and persons producing a related product in the country who wanted to extend their product range (two cases).

Of the seventeen firms responding to an outside stimulus the remaining ten responded to an actual imposition of a tariff, quota provision or licence system by the government of the country to which they were exporting, or responded to a belief

The preliminary stages

> **Scenario 4.2.1** Success rating: '1'
>
> In 1968 a small firm in the South-East of England was heavily involved with a large multinational firm, and had earned ten per cent bonuses on work for delivery ahead of agreed dates. As a result of this good work the firm was made known to a major operating subsidiary of the multinational, and that subsidiary promised work if the firm established a production unit in Belgium. The firm did so in 1973; initially orders were supplied but they failed to materialise with sufficient regularity or volume and the plant was closed after eighteen months. Paradoxically, a similar venture in Norway began after a similar response and led to the firm's second overseas production subsidiary, the profits of which covered the losses on the Belgian operation.

or threat that a tariff, quota provision or licence system would be imposed. The firms believed that as a result exports would fall and only a production subsidiary in the country, that is an operation behind the tariff or other protective wall, could preserve the market share of the firm and thus they set up the subsidiary. The average success rating for the overseas production subsidiaries was 1.9, as shown in Table 4.3. Among the subsidiaries there was none rated as 'totally successful' but examples of the other four ratings were found. In five of the ten cases the country involved was South Africa and the average rating was 2.6; in two cases the country involved was Australia and both subsidiaries were rated '1'. The relevant point here is that Australia never imposed the threatened trade barriers whereas South Africa did and the difference in success ratings presumably reflects the very real protection that can be offered to a small production subsidiary by a trade barrier.

This short section has covered the experiences of those

seventeen firms which set up their first overseas production subsidiaries in response to an outside stimulus. Two lessons appear from two very different outside stimuli: approaches by persons outside of the firm need vetting carefully and a trade barrier offers effective protection to a production subsidiary.

4.3 Other primary motivations

Responses to enquiries on motivation, other than those covered in the preceding section can be termed as 'push' or 'pull' motivations. The push motivation is concerned with the economic, political and social conditions in the UK as perceived by the senior managers of the firm which lead them to prefer to invest overseas. Pull motivation is concerned with the attractions of the foreign country for investment purposes.

Table 4.4 shows the responses, other than those covered in the preceding section, to the question: 'What was the single most important factor that led your firm to make its first foreign investment in production facilities?'. The twenty-six responses are split into push motivations (two firms) and pull motivations (twenty-four firms).

Paradoxically, for the two responses which can be categorised as push motives for the establishment of an overseas production subsidiary, the views of the UK firms represented are quite different. One firm invested overseas as a way of transferring capital out of the UK, and as much of the profits as possible were to be kept overseas. The plant was put into West Germany, the main export market — thus while 'push' was the reason for going overseas, the plant was actually located by a 'pull' factor (the market the firm already had in West Germany). On the rating scheme set up in Chapter 3, this overseas production subsidiary was rated '2', an average success, but of course to the firm it is in a sense a much greater success since the owner-manager's view of the UK was that there was little future for the private firm in the UK. The view

Table 4.4

What was the single most important factor that led your firm to make its first foreign investment in production facilities?

Response	Number of firms	Mean success rating
Of the two firms citing 'push' factors:		
'To get capital out of the UK'	1	2.0
'Already making good profits in UK, little further scope'	1	0
	2	1.0
Of the twenty-four firms citing 'pull' factors:		
'To enable us to compete effectively with local firms'	6	2.8
'There is a large market overseas'	5	2.4
'To get a production base in the EEC'	8	2.2
'UK market absorbs all our UK production and so foreign markets have to be supplied from elsewhere'	1	2.0
'So our product will be associated with one manufactured there'	1	2.0
'The export tax relief available there'	1	2.0
'The materials supplies are located there'	1	2.0
'The necessary labour was available there and not here'	1	1.0
	24	2.3

of the UK of the other firm was different The firm was so successful in the UK that it could see no room for further growth, and accordingly widened its horizons and invested overseas. However, the best the overseas production subsidiary ever achieved before it closed, was a loss of £30 000 in one year. The rating is '0'. There seems to be no lessons here for other managers since the causes of lack of success were related to factors other than the 'push' from the UK.

In terms of 'pull' motivations, there were twenty-four firms and the specific motivations are shown in the lower part of Table 4.4. There are six firms whose primary motivation in setting up an overseas production subsidiary was to enable

> **Scenario 4.3.1**   Success rating: '2'
>
> A firm in the general area of light engineering, run by an entrepreneur, opened its first overseas production subsidiary in West Germany in 1973. The response to Question 5 of the questionnaire (see page 232) was to the effect that the more money he could get out of the UK the better, that the UK was now suspect in certain areas, for example privately-owned firms, and that if the overseas production subsidiary and the two subsequent ones could generate sufficient cash, he could leave the UK altogether. In respect of subsidiary motives, the response was that the German plant was a good insurance against trades union action at the UK plant.

them to compete effectively with local firms. The reasoning was that a local production unit would have no transport costs from the UK to the local market, that the local customers would see theplant as a sign of faith and goodwill in their country, and that the product could be adapted exactly to local requirements. Looking at the success ratings associated with these six firms, it is important to note that there were two 'totally successful' ventures and no ventures rated as 'not successful' or 'failure' — giving the group an overall mean rating of 2.8.

Another common response was to the effect that a large market existed overseas, for example: 'We were aware that the market there (in the USA) is some ten times the size of the UK and our machines are in advance of most in terms of technology'. The problem with this kind of statement is of course that there is inherent in the statement no reason why the US market could not be supplied from the UK; but, of course, subsequent questions in the interview went on to determine the reasons. (Part of the reason in this case was that the product specification was different for the US market and a production unit there could produce to, and keep abreast of, local product specifications.) The mean success rating of the five firms citing this reason is 2.4 and there were no 'failures' in this group.

The distinct pull factor of the EEC is the most common response in Table 4.4. Eight firms felt this pull and a response from one firm typical of these eight is: 'We felt we must try to get into Europe; we had tried exporting, direct selling, agents, etc., which were not as successful as we wanted. We then realised that local manufacturing facilities werenecessary so that everything could be made to market requirements.' While the mean success rating is just above average at 2.2, there is the complete range of outcomes for the eight firms which means that caution is needed for any firm currently feeling the pull of the EEC.

The remainder of Table 4.4 lists single-occurrence responses to the question on motivation and to complete this section Table 4.5 lists the responses to the subsidiary question: 'Will you now tell me what subsidiary (motivational) factors were important in that first foreign venture?'. In brief, the secondary motives reinforce the primary motives noted above; and motives relating to the market again predominate, with the need to adapt the product to local conditions and tastes being best fulfilled by an overseas production subsidiary occurring in nine cases. Perhaps also the increased occurrence of 'push' factors should be noted, perhaps their listing is of secondary importance which indicates that they linger under the surface in this and other investment decisions.

This section has attempted to establish the motives which led to the decision to set up an overseas production subidiary. As in any complex decision, there must be a blurring of motives, and these may be coloured by later events. However, in asking the questions relating to primary and secondary motives, and in subsequent general discussion, it is likely that on balance the real motives were determined. This section has analysed those motives and related them to the level of success

Table 4.5

Will you now tell me, what subsidiary (motivational) factors were important in that first foreign venture?

Response	Number of firms*	Mean success rating
1. External approaches	5	1.8
2. Push factors:		
transport cost/delivery problems from UK	4	1.5
ancillary cost problems in UK;	1	3.0
to avoid manufacturing in UK (union problems)	1	2.0
no further expansion in UK for tax reasons	1	2.0
fear of UK Monopolies Commission	1	0
3. Pull factors:		
the size of the market	13	2.2
the need for local adaption, or resident production	9	2.2
to get a European production base	5	1.4
to ensure exports of intermediate goods	4	2.0
'it's a nice country'	3	2.0
room for expansion	3	1.7
personal/family links	3	1.7
tariff/import licences	2	3.0
to compete effectively with locals	2	1.5
to get access to skilled foreign management	1	4.0
to ensure supplies of inputs	1	3.0
to get access to host government contracts	1	3.0
to have a factory in Commonwealth	1	3.0
access to foreign technology	1	2.0
host country grants	1	2.0
had to manufacture to maintain patents	1	0

* Number sums more than forty-three due to multiple responses.

achieved by the overseas production subsidiaries that resulted from those motives. While the evidence is not extensive, it does appear that motivation based on 'push' factors (basically a desire to produce outside of the UK) does not lead to a successful overseas production subsidiary. However, 'pull' motivations predominated in the forty-three firms analysed

> **Scenario 4.3.2** Success rating: '4'
>
> The primary motive for this firm, a small firm specialising in one part of the electronics field, in opening an overseas production subsidiary in West Germany was that the German market was twice the size of the UK. It had established this as a result of its exporting there from 1958 onwards and from its overseas sales subsidiary set up in 1970. In 1973 it began production in West Germany. No subsidiary motives (see Question 6, page 232) were important in the decision.

here and key pull factors, in the sense that the subsequent overseas production subsidiaries tended to be successful, are the desires to compete and to produce locally in order to convince local customers of good intentions and to supply exactly those products in local demand.

4.4 Selection of country

In the preliminary stages of going international a decision has to be made as to in which country the overseas production subsidiary is to be sited. Given the wide choice of countries and given the dangers involved in investing overseas, it is surprising that only fifteen of the forty-three firms in the survey at any stage considered an alternative country to the one in which they in fact established their first overseas production. This finding resulted from questions which requested information as to whether alternative countries were considered, which ones, and for how long they were under consideration.

Table 4.6 shows the success ratings for the fifteen firms which did consider alternative countries, and compares them with the other twenty-eight which homed-in immediately on the one country for the siting of their first overseas production subsidiary. On average there is no difference between the success ratings; this does not allow one to conclude that the search procedure is of no value. One reason is that if the firms

Table 4.6

Did you look at any alternative countries?

Response	Number of firms	Mean success rating
Yes	15	2.1
No	28	2.0
	43	

which did look at alternatives had not done so, they may on average have done worse than the group of firms which homed-in straight away to the one country. The other reason is that the firms which did home-in immediately to one country had perhaps little choice (for example, that country was by far their biggest export market) and by intuition rather than deliberate search had limited themselves to the one possible country.

Among the fifteen which did do a search were the two which indicated 'push' factors as their primary motivation for investing outside the UK, and among the fifteen the search for alternative countries was in twelve cases restricted wholly to the EEC, and in the three remaining cases, restricted wholly to the 'White Dominions' — hence the search area was preselected, in exactly the same way presumably as the other twenty-eight firms preselected the country of investment. Of the twelve making an EEC search, three finally went to their largest export market and three to the country in which their best agent operated.

The search for alternatives was not a long process; two to six months was usual, and twelve months the longest search period. This presumably reflects the ever-present scarcity of

> **Scenario 4.4.1**   Success rating: '1'
>
> Before opening up an overseas production subsidiary in West Germany in 1956, the firm considered West Germany, France, Belgium, Italy and Holland. The exports to these countries amounted to forty-seven per cent of the total exports, and the primary motivation in opening an overseas production subsidiary was to be able to service these export markets. On the basis of the extensive travels associated with exporting, and clearly extensive knowledge of the industry in each of the countries, France and Italy were ruled out on the basis of their business ethics being unsatisfactory to this firm; a site on the Rhine in Holland was regarded as an ideal spot as this could service both Holland and Germany. However, the choice for the first overseas production subsidiary went to Germany on the grounds that Germany was the biggest single market, and the site on the Rhine became the place for the second production subsidiary which now services Holland and backs-up the German plant for the German market.

managerial time in small firms and the high cost to a small firm of a systematic review of alternative countries.

Perhaps the most appropriate comment in this short section is to warn of the two dangers which stand out when the search process is limited. The first is the danger of seizing too soon on to a proposal from abroad — the first agent to give you the idea may not be in the best country for your plant, and he may not be the best partner or manager — and the second danger is to enter too soon into a *commitment*, which gathers its own momentum and an overseas production subsidiary is set up before anyone in the firm really takes a positive decision.

4.5 Country of location

It was shown in the preceding section that firms typically home-in on the host country for their investment very quickly, and hence it is legitimate to look at the country of location as a preliminary to the investment, rather than as part of the planning process (Chapter 5) or the investment itself (Chapter 6). In this section it is proposed to examine briefly the success of the first overseas production subsidiaries country by country. The data are assembled in Table 4.7.

South Africa was not only the single most popular country but it also achieved the highest mean success rating. West Germany follows closely behind in popularity and with equal

Table 4.7 Country of location

Country	Number of firms	Mean success rating
South Africa	9	2.8
West Germany	8	2.8
Australia	6	2.0
Eire	4	1.8
Holland	4	1.8
Belgium and Luxembourg	6	1.7
USA	2	2.0
Norway	1	2.0
France	2	0
Italy	1	0
	43	

success. Australia then follows with a mean success rating of exactly 'average success' for the six firms which opened their first overseas production subsidiary there. In all three countries there is an absence of 'failures' and the three countries cover just over half of the sample of forty-three ventures. The mean success rating for the three countries is 2.6, which compares with the mean rating of 1.5 for the twenty ventures in other countries.

Too much emphasis must not be placed on these data — for example, the conclusion cannot be reached that for any given firm it would do better to go to South Africa rather than France or Italy, but a conclusion that some countries, in particular South Africa, West Germany and Australia, clearly and repeatedly have tended to be the location of successful ventures, is in order. On these grounds, those countries need to be considered by a firm contemplating going international.

If the data are rearranged by putting the countries into trading blocs, then fifteen of the first overseas production subsidiaries went to the White Dominions (here in fact Australia and South Africa), twenty-one to the EEC (here in fact just the 'six' old members) and seven to the rest of the world. The data relating to success are shown in Table 4.8,

Table 4.8 Trading bloc location

Trading bloc	Number of firms	Mean success rating
White Dominions	15	2.5
EEC (Old 'Six')	21	1.9
Other	7	1.9
	43	

while the EEC and the rest of the world have the same mean success rating, the 'White Dominion' areas have a higher mean success rating.

Looking at the range of success underlying the averages shown in the tables, it seems that the greatest pay-offs and the biggest failures have both occurred within the EEC. Only six overseas production subsidiaries out of the forty-three were rated as totally successful, and four of these were established in the EEC (two in Germany, one in Holland and one in Luxembourg)[*]; on the other hand all of the five rated as failures were EEC based (two in France, one each in Italy, Belgium and Holland). One reading of the interviews is that firms which were better prepared and ready to accept the challenges of establishing an overseas production subsidiary in Europe can achieve a high pay-off, but those which are less

---
[*]The other two were in South Africa.

well prepared and cannot command the requisite resources can meet with very serious consequences as a result of competition inside the EEC.

This point can be amplified in terms of the risks involved. Most UK managers would regard entry into the EEC by setting up an overseas production subsidiary as a far more risky venture than an equivalent project in the White Dominions, because the culture and language between the UK and its former colonies are very similar, and there is an established tradition of economic intercourse, often reinforced by kinship ties. Many managers would probably feel that the 'political' risks are lower also (although this assessment of South Africa may be undergoing change). Consequently, one interpretation is that the more risk-averse firms establish their first overseas production subsidiaries in the developed Commonwealth, while the more risk-accepting firms take their chances in the EEC, and the levels of success and failure reflect this choice.

The pattern of preference for the White Dominions vis-à-vis the EEC has changed, as can be seen from Table 4.9. Period by period, one area rather than another has been favoured.

Table 4.9 Trading bloc and date of establishment

Overseas production subsidiaries opened in:

Date	White Dominions	EEC	Other
1948-60	4	5	3
1961-65	7	3	1
1966-70	3	5	2
1971-75	1	8	1
	15	21	7

The fluctuations in numbers of subsidiaries established appear to be EEC in origin in the sense that the EEC was favoured either when it was thought the UK would join the EEC, or when the common external tariff of the Six became a problem to UK firms. The EEC has obviously been identified by many firms as the target area for the 1970s — especially as all of the 'eight' firms, shown in Table 4.9 as 1970-5, have set up their overseas production subsidiaries in the EEC since the UK's entry in 1973. The challenge and prospects of the EEC, as noted at several points, brings great problems of adaptation of product, methods and beliefs to local conditions; these represent a major area of risk in investing in the EEC, and a clear lesson from the interviews is that a small UK firm has to adapt to the local conditions or it will fail.

This section has looked at how success varies depending upon the country in which the overseas production subsidiary is located. Success does vary markedly country by country. While some care must be exercised in reaching conclusions because only forty-three firms have been analysed the rate of success is higher in South Africa, West Germany and Australia than elsewhere. In particular it appears that changes in product or managerial outlook are less necessary in South Africa and Australia than in EEC countries, tilting the balance of success toward the overseas production subsidiaries in the White Dominions. In the EEC high success is frequent but so too is total failure. The small UK firm must match its own willingness to take risks and to change its products and ideas with the data and comments in this section in order to further its own chances of being successful when it opens its first overseas production subsidiary.

Executive summary

In this chapter, the first to look at some of the characteristics the overseas production subsidiaries in relation to their levels of success, the emphasis has been upon the preliminary stages of the investment. Thus the chapter has looked at the route to production overseas (Section 4.1), the impact of an outside stimulus (Section 4.2), the primary motivation for the investment (Section 4.3), selection of country (Section 4.4), and (Section 4.5), the countries in which the investments were made. In each case, the overseas production subsidiaries have been classified by their success ratings.

In respect of the route to the overseas production subsidiary, the experiences of the forty-three firms in Section 4.1 tended to confirm common business sense. A variety of routes is possible, the most direct going straight to the establishment of an overseas production subsidiary based solely on the experiences of UK operations. Less direct routes involve intermediate steps such as exporting, using a foreign agent for export selling, and operating an overseas sales subsidiary, and one or all of these intermediate steps is possible. On average, success went to those firms using the longer routes, the inference is that each step gives information to the firm, represents an opportunity for reassessing the overall strategy and forms a base from which the next step can be taken.

As well as success tending to go to those firms using the longer routes, success tends to go to those firms with more extensive experience of the market; thus those firms with a higher proportion of sales going to the host country tend to have more success with their first overseas production subsidiary in that country.

The empirical evidence and common business sense therefore suggest a clear strategy for those firms wishing to establish an overseas production subsidiary — it is to proceed step by step by means of exports, an agent and an overseas sales subsidiary, and at each step to build and nurture the market in that country and then set up the overseas production subsidiary.

This strategy was denied to the firms in Section 4.2 which responded quickly to an outside stimulus, for example the threat of a tariff wall or an approach by a person external to the firm. The lessons here are that production operations inside a tariff wall do tend to be successful, but extreme care is needed in responding to an approach from a person outside the firm.

In terms of motivation for setting up an overseas production subsidiary, Section 4.3 showed the primary motivation was a 'pull' from overseas markets in general or one market in particular. One reading of the situation is that the best gains are made when there is a specific reason for locating in a particular market. This should be interpreted not simply as the largest export market for the firm, although this is important, but it should be ascertained that the customers in that country are likely to respond positively to the firm committing money and resources to their country by opening an overseas production subsidiary.

In Section 4.4 only one third of the firms considered countries other than the one in which they did locate their first overseas production subsidiary and on average, success neither favoured nor disfavoured either group of firms — perhaps because the search was often preconditioned by the outside stimulus or approach, or by the fact that the country was the largest export market.

The country of location, in Section 4.5, proved to be a critical factor. There has been a preference for the White Dominions (South Africa and Australia) and overseas production subsidiaries there have tended to be successful. West Germany is the only other country which can match the success of these two countries. Of course, the fact that overseas production subsidiaries have been successful in these three countries does not mean necessarily that future overseas production subsidiaries should be located there since, for example, the comments in the preceding paragraph might indicate a location for an overseas production subsidiary outside of these three countries.

Preference for the White Dominions has fluctuated over time as events in the EEC unfolded, and overseas production subsidiaries in the EEC appear to be the most successful or the largest failures, and it is likely that the firm considering production inside the EEC needs to exercise more care than one considering investing in the White Dominions, but the indications are that with care the biggest success may come in the EEC.

Several critical factors have been identified in this chapter and managers considering an overseas production subsidiary should build on the experiences of the forty-three firms surveyed here in order to tilt the balance toward success and avoid failures of a magnitude which can threaten the survival of the UK operations.

5 The planning stages

While the title of this chapter might convey the impression that the forty-three firms, after the preliminaries discussed in Chapter 4, settled down to a planning and evaluation phase prior to a decision, it is legitimate to point out that many of the firms had, at this stage, already made the decision to invest in their first overseas production subsidiary. For some, this was a conscious decision, albeit reached quickly and at an early stage without careful evaluation of the facts. For many, however, the decision was probably not conscious in the sense that the process simply gathered its own momentum, and the result was the establishment of an overseas production subsidiary. Indeed, in some cases, it was difficult to see at what stage prior to the first actual production coming off the line, did someone in the firm sit down and make a conscious decision. The inability to see that decision in some cases does not, however, invalidate the layout of these five chapters into the preliminary stages, the planning stages, the investment stages, control, and lessons and problems, since these represent a logical time sequence in their own right.

This chapter, the planning stages, looks at the choice between one hundred per cent or joint ventures, takeovers versus greenfield ventures, planning procedures viewed with the benefit of hindsight, information gathering, market research, and visits overseas by managers of the firm. As in the previous chapter, and in the subsequent two, the theme is to relate these factors to the success ratings of the overseas production subsidiaries, and in the process hopefully convey to managers of other small firms the benefits of, and lessons from, the experiences of the small firms in this survey.

5.1 Ownership strategy

In the cases where the stimulus to set up an overseas production subsidiary was the result of a person approaching the firm, it is natural that the person would expect some share in the venture. And, in the cases where the motivation arose within the firm, the firm's existing contacts (for example, the agent) in the country in which the overseas production subsidiary was to be established were often included in the venture. In this short section the purpose is simply to compare the overseas production subsidiaries where one hundred per cent control was held by the firm and the overseas production subsidiaries where the firm held less than one hundred per cent control (joint ventures).

The categories chosen were 'one hundred per cent control', 'seventy-five to ninety-nine per cent control' (seventy-five per cent being a minimum for certain 'special resolutions' in company affairs), 'fifty-one to seventy-four per cent control' (fifty-one per cent ensuring sufficient votes for most 'ordinary resolutions'), and 'fifty per cent or less' (to represent those situations where the firm is forced into a co-operative posture because it is managing the venture with other persons with equal or greater voting power). The number of firms in each category is shown in Table 5.1. Most firms were in the one hundred per cent category, and compared with the twenty-four firms in that category there were only eight in the seventy-five to ninety-nine per cent category and eight in the fifty per cent or less category, leaving three in the fifty-one to seventy-four per cent category. The success ratings are shown in the table and the mean for the one hundred per cent group is 2.2, only slightly above 'average success', but the mean for the seventy-five to ninety-nine per cent category is higher at 2.6.

Table 5.1

What percentage of ownership did you have in the venture?

Response	Number of firms	Mean success rating
100%	24	2.2
75-99%	8	2.6
51-74%	3	1.3
50% or less	8	1.6
	43	
Absolute control	32	2.3
Less than absolute control	11	1.5
	43	

The means for the two categories of firms with less than seventy-five per cent control are 1.3 for fifty-one to seventy-four per cent and 1.6 for fifty per cent or less. If the two categories with absolute control are combined (that is, all firms with seventy-five per cent or more of the voting power) the overall average success rating is 2.3, to be compared with an overall average of 1.5 for the firms with less than absolute control.

Again, the warning must be issued that the sample size is small and the number in any category in a table may be very small, so that the success ratings may be influenced unduly by chance; and accordingly no definite statistical conclusions can be reached. However, the treatment of each table is to take it as part of an overall picture of success and failure, and with this treatment, Table 5.1 suggests that part of the picture for success lies with having control of the venture.

The arguments for and against one hundred per cent control, and having a local partner in the venture, probably set the scene most usefully for others having to make the decision in the near future.

> **Scenario 5.1.1** Success rating: '1'
>
> A UK firm employing eighty people and operating in a part of the heavy metals industry opened an overseas production unit in Belgium in 1975. It was a fifty/fifty venture with a Swiss firm. Initially the UK firm had hoped for a US partner to gain its technical expertise, but it fell through because the US firm wanted a majority holding. It failed too to find a Belgian partner which would have had the local knowledge, and in the end went ahead with the Swiss firm. However, precisely the problems where a local partner could have helped occurred, in particular problems about conflicting demands in planning permission between provincial and communal planning bodies, and about the size of investment inducements to which the overseas production subsidiary was entitled — in fact none had been received by the date of the interview. And, in this case as a bonus problem in the fifty/fifty situation, the changing values of the pound sterling, Belgian franc and Swiss franc upset the financial basis of the venture.

In favour of one hundred per cent is the simple fact that control is complete; there is no other person to convince of the 'rightness' of a decision or change in policy. Less time is spent in reaching a decision and in implementing it. Such views were expressed frequently and often strongly by people interviewed in the survey whose first overseas production subsidiary had been a joint venture but in subsequent ones had formed a policy of wholly-owned ventures only. Against one hundred per cent control is an equally simple argument that the whole risk is being borne by the one firm. This argument had particular relevance for one firm whose Australian subsidiary required more cash than anticipated. The firm did not have the extra money but the partner did, and put up the money. As a result, the (UK) firm's holding went down from fifty per cent to twenty-four per cent, but the overseas production subsidiary is rated as 'very successful', and twenty-four per cent of 'very successful' may be better than one hundred per cent of a cash-starved overseas production subsidiary.

Joint ventures allow the partner to bring in local knowledge, and this may be particularly valuable in a first overseas production subsidiary, when the firm has no previous overseas experience to draw upon. Local knowledge of operating conditions, labour laws, factory regulations, customers and marketing methods are essential to the overseas production subsidiary, and a local partner may be the cheapest way of getting this knowledge. Perhaps the most important local knowledge a partner can bring is that of the short cuts, knowing just who in which particular ministry or local government department has the power to authorise something. A persistent element of surprise to UK managers setting up their first overseas production subsidiaries was that the traditional English civil servant, who may be disliked in the UK for his desire to follow rules, has no counterpart in some overseas countries — there may be no rules, giving the civil servant absolute discretion over a decision, and cash may be a necessary feature of a decision. Another advantage of a joint venture is the risk-sharing element noted in the previous paragraph, and again in some countries the host government may look with favour only upon ventures which have some local involvement. The favour may be expressed in the form of grants or, just as importantly, smoothing the way through the bureaucracy. Finally, of course, a possible advantage is that the local partner may be a good manager!

On balance, the overseas production subsidiaries which were set up as joint ventures are the ones in which problems were emphasised in the course of the interviews, and it may be worthwhile noting that the two overseas production subsidiaries rated as 'totally successful' were initially joint ventures, but after a time the local partner was bought out to give the UK firms the one hundred per cent control seen as necessary for the continuance of their overseas operations.

In summary, Table 5.1 shows that firms which had control in the range of seventy-five to ninety-nine per cent achieved the highest mean success rating. This supports the general comments above because it combines *de facto* control in all situations with the benefit of local participation and knowledge. Failing such minority local participation, the evidence suggests that one hundred per cent control is the preferred degree of ownership.

5.2 Takeovers versus greenfield ventures

A local partner can be involved whether the overseas production subsidiary is the result of a takeover of an ongoing local venture, or the result of a greenfield operation (where the entrant firm obtains or hires land, factory, machinery and men and begins a totally new operation). Where the entry into the country is via a takeover, some, all or none of the existing managers or owners can be retained — equally in a greenfield venture, the firm's existing agent or a customer or other business contact may be brought into the venture. This section examines the importance of the choice of takeover or greenfield venture and its impact on success.

A firm often has a preconceived idea of which form of entry it would prefer. Table 5.2 shows the intitial preferences which were two-thirds to one-third for greenfield ventures

Table 5.2

When you first decided to invest in . . . what kind of investment did you want to make?

Response	Number of firms
A greenfield venture	28
A takeover	15
	43

over takeovers. Typical comments effectively summarise the general arguments. In expressing its preference for greenfield, one firm regarded it as the only possible way for a small firm because they assumed it was cheaper, since if they took over a good firm it would be expensive, and if they took over a bad firm the price would be low but all the firm's faults and problems would be inherited. Other firms stressed the lack of choice they faced in takeover possibilities, since there were so few firms of their size in the industry in the host country. Given the fact that the survey was concerned with smaller firms, with

---

Scenario 5.2.1   Success rating: '2'

A small private limited company in the general field of heating began an overseas production subsidiary in West Germany in 1968. Demand for its products in the UK was taking all the output of the UK plant and it was decided to supply the main export market in West Germany from a plant there. The preference from the start was for a greenfield venture 'probably because this is a private company which cherishes its independence'. Further reasons were, however, that in Europe only a few companies make the product (in fact, a small component with wide use in heating systems) and in West Germany there was only one manufacturer — and the desire was to be in direct competition with him, rather than to buy him out.

---

their feelings of independence, it was not surprising that some preferred greenfield ventures because 'we wanted to start it off our way'.

However, preference for takeover as a method of entry was also found among the survey firms. Thus takeover was the established growth policy for some firms; others wished to add new products to the existing range, and others assumed that a lot of capital and a lot of time were necessary for greenfield ventures so that a quicker return on capital would be obtained by takeover. (While this view is contradictory to one in the previous paragraph, both are equally valid as general *a priori* statements; in a single situation, however, some quick calculations could establish which was cheaper or quicker.) The strongest preference for takeover was usually expressed in the form 'we were buying the most valuable asset of all — management'. (In fact, the firm quoted in this case was rated as '1' on our success scale, but almost the same words were used by one rated as '4'.) In general, the advantages of takeover revolve around the fact that it *is* the purchase of an existing concern and that fact should enable the firm to circumvent many cultural, legal and management problems, and in particular start-up problems are avoided. The existing

---

Scenario 5.2.2   Success rating: '3'

A firm making small electrical appliances set up an overseas production subsidiary in West Germany in 1967 in response to a feeling that it would be more economical to supply the market from there, and a feeling that their products would become more acceptable to their German customers if they were manufactured there. The entry was via the greenfield method — 'there were few people to take over but we couldn't afford to buy anybody anyway. We invested damn all (less than £10 000); just dipped our hands into petty cash; we really invested our time and energy.' Some indication of the abilities of this firm fully to utilise scarce resources can be seen when it is pointed out that both of the firm's overseas sales subsidiaries initially operated from the basements of the homes of the men in charge of those subsidiaries.

---

management will have shown its ability, and if that ability is high the managers will be familiar with the unit's problems and potential. The drawbacks, if they are not carefully planned for, are however, huge. One problem is the possibility of over-payment, either because the price of each element of the purchased firm is often upped by a small amount, which together add up to a considerable premium, or because it is difficult to value the unit as a part of a UK operation. Second, there are the problems of integrating a unit with its own ethics, beliefs, control procedures and established methods into a foreign (UK-owned) firm with its own attitudes and methods. Lastly, there is the management time involved in the search procedure, the negotiations and the takeover period, which can be as prolonged as the time it takes to set up a greenfield venture.

Almost all the firms kept to their initial preferences but one firm which wanted to enter the host country by takeover was unable to do so because it could not find a firm with the required characteristics. Therefore a greenfield venture was made. As a result, the number of firms in Table 5.3 showing the actual route is little changed from Table 5.2. The mean success ratings for the forty-three firms are shown in Table 5.3 and the outcome of the allocation of the overseas production

Table 5.3

In the outcome, what type of investment did you make?

Response	Number of firms	Mean success rating
A greenfield venture	29	2.1
A takeover	14	2.0
	43	

subsidiaries according to their method of entry in terms of success ratings is quite clear. All the ratings of success are found with both methods of entry, no pattern exists and the success ratings for each method are approximately equal.

A pattern does appear however when Table 5.3 is broken down by method of entry (greenfield or takeover) and the percentage control in the venture. The reworked table is

Table 5.4. It suggests (as in the previous section) that success is related to the degree of control and method of entry is not critical. Thus the table shows that where control was seventy-five per cent or more of the voting power then mean success

Table 5.4 Control and method of entry

	Number of firms	Mean success rating
Greenfield with control of 75% or more	23	2.2
Takeover with control of 75% or more	8	2.3
Greenfield with control or 74% or less	6	1.7
Takeover with control of 74% or less	6	1.7

was about equal for both greenfield and takeover. Where control was less, mean success was lower at 1.7 for both.

On the basis of Tables 5.3 and 5.4 the conclusion must be that, on average, the method of entry to the market is not a major factor in the success of the venture. However, on the basis of the interviews, the conclusion is a more forceful one. It is that the preconceived idea of whether a takeover or a greenfield venture is the better method of entry was so strongly expressed that in most cases no consideration whatsoever was given to the alternative method, much less any rudimentary analysis of the costs or time scale of the alternative. In fact, it appears that in only one case was the alternative investigated, and this was where the firm was unable to find a suitable company for takeover, and was forced into a greenfield method of entry. Interestingly, that firm was rated as 'totally successful'.

5.3 With the benefit of hindsight

The very last question in the interview was designed to be open-ended, to give the interviewee a chance to cover any

The planning stages 79

points not covered elsewhere — and, of course, some of the most illuminating information came at this point. Many of the comments have been used where they seem appropriate; in this section the intention is to report the 'narrow' answers to this last question: 'With the benefit of hindsight, knowing what you know now, how would you do it differently if you were setting about it today?'.

Alarmingly, the most common answer, which came from eleven firms, was that they would do it no differently today even with the benefit of hindsight! A liberal interpretation is simply one of smugness. In one case, this may be true, the overseas production subsidiary was rated as 'totally successful' and it had been a smooth and, clearly, a professionally-managed operation. That one apart, however, it must be noted that of the remaining ten, no fewer than nine were rated 'average' or 'not successful'. These were the operations which on the criteria laid down in Chapter 4 (overseas profitability vis-à-vis UK profitability, the firm's own perceptions of success — both subjectively and objectively measured, growth — both achieved and planned, the willingness to invest overseas after the first venture, and the performance of exports subsequent to the establishment of the overseas production subsidiary) could not be described as other than 'average' or 'not successful'. It is perhaps instructive that there were no respondents whose overseas production subsidiary got a '0' rating who said that they would do it no differently today.

Those firms apart, the major grouping of positive responses relates to the management of the operation itself. Four firms noted that they would go more slowly and give themselves more time on each decision, and two noted they should have gone in at a larger scale of operations. These responses and others are shown in Table 5.5. To an extent it is important that firms thinking of setting up an overseas production subsidiary study Table 5.5 with some care, because it is the catch-all for problems encountered and lessons learned not covered explicitly in other sections.

The next grouping in the table related to managerial

> **Scenario 5.3.1** Success rating: '2'
>
> Prices in the industry are quoted on a 'delivered-site' basis and to facilitate quotations on this basis the firm set up an overseas production subsidiary in Belgium in 1974. The chief executive was British and language turned out to be a big problem. With the benefit of hindsight the firm would have found a local man, and taught him English if necessary, rather than using a Briton and attempting to teach him Flemish. Also with the benefit of hindsight, the firm would allow a longer period to break even — the overseas production subsidiary had not made profits to the date of the interview, and the respondent admitted that it was unrealistic of him to have expected any so soon. As a final change, if the firm was allowed to do the whole operation again knowing what they now know, they would take more care in training the shop-floor workers. They had assumed, incorrectly, that in that part of Belgium they could, as in their area of the UK, simply recruit people from the employment office already familiar with the basic production skills the firm required. The firm realised that the same problem would have existed if they had attempted to set up production in the UK away from the traditional areas of production of their product.

problems. Thus three firms were convinced on the basis of their experience that the top man should have been a national of the host country instead of a Briton sent out from the UK. This point, local versus Briton, was the one point in the survey on which the most deeply expressed views were held, and on balance no affirmative decision can be reached by the survey. The argument in favour of a Briton is that he knows the UK operations and can manage the overseas production subsidiary

Table 5.5

With the benefit of hindsight, knowing what you know now, how would you do it differently, if you were setting about it today?

Primary response	Number of firms
No differently	11
Go more slowly	4
Go in at a larger scale	2
Recognise and correct mistakes more quickly	1
Think more about the longer-term effects	1
Be more aware of national characteristics, customs, etc.	1
Top man must be a local	3
Send out UK managers, rather than use locals	2
Be more selective in choice of men sent from UK	2
Need a management team, wrong to rely on one man	2
Be more selective in local recruiting	1
Have one hundred per cent control	2
Spend more time getting financial details of relationship with partner right	2
Go in as a minority shareholder	1
Realise that setting up an overseas production subsidiary was the wrong strategy	6
Do not rely on freelance salesmen	1
Send best plant, rather than second-hand plant	1
	43

in a manner that is fully consistent with the objectives and philosophies of the UK firm and will communicate in words and figures that are in line with UK thinking. For the local, the argument is precisely the reverse; the overseas production subsidiary is in his own country and he will manage the overseas production subsidiary in a manner that is fully consistent with the objectives and philosophies of the host country. However, and to many firms this is the crunch, he will communicate in words and figures that even in English may not carry the same connotations as he intends or the UK managers perceive. While not being able to judge this issue on the basis of the experiences of the forty-three firms in the survey, the view might be taken that *good* chief executives are so hard to find, that the search ought to be for a good one, and to keep him once identified, irrespective of nationality.

Table 5.5 is supplemented by Table 5.6 and both are presented, not in the usual fashion of relating key factors to eventual success or failure, but in the fashion of information

Table 5.6

With the benefit of hindsight, knowing what you know now, how would you do it differently, if you were setting about it today?

Secondary response	Number of firms
Control whole operation more carefully	2
Do more planning	1
Don't try with a new product	1
Build it up more gradually	1
Allow longer to break even	1
Time entry better	1
Move faster	1
Top men must be local	1
Have one hundred per cent control	1

that at the planning stages of an overseas production subsidiary should give the firm some pointers as to how those who have already set up an overseas production subsidiary would now do that same operation.

The two tables in this section taken together with Table 8.8 and Table 8.9 should be treated as an essential checklist by a manager somewhere along the path from the initial idea of having an overseas production subsidiary to the eventual operation of that subsidiary. The checklist is essential simply because the items are those picked out quite freely by managers who have taken that same path.

5.4 Further information required

Table 4.1 showed the route to an overseas production subsidiary taken by each of the forty-three firms in the survey;

thirty-six firms had had some experience of the country in which they eventually located their first overseas production subsidiary. The experience of these firms has been gained through exporting and having an agent or having a sales subsidiary in that country, and was based often on a considerable period of time. This accumulated experience was obviously a foundation in the decision to establish an overseas production subsidiary, but to determine what additional information was most important in the planning stage, the question was asked: 'What was the single most important piece of information required about . . ., other than accumulated experience, before you took the final decision?'. The responses are in Table 5.7.

In Table 5.7 nine firms investigated the market further to add to their accumulated experience of the local market and the mean level of success was 2.6; all nine firms being rated 'average success' or higher. To a question such as this diverse answers can be expected; but a large number of firms — fifteen out of the forty-three — said they required no additional information. For the fifteen the mean rating was low, 1.7, that rating being augmented considerably by the inclusion of two 'totally successful' overseas production subsidiaries. One of these included a response to the effect that the initial investment was only £2 500 and 'we would not lose out if the venture failed' — rationalising, this statment implies that the cost of getting additional information could exceed the cost of the investment. The other of the two had been operating an overseas sales subsidiary for three years and knew West Germany 'must be a good market, it's a thriving industrial country, there is no German manufacturer and we already manufacture (in the UK) to German specifications'. Other responses are detailed in Table 5.7 and are fairly diverse, as anticipated.

In general the responses in Table 5.7 indicate to the firm currently considering investing in an overseas production subsidiary a useful checklist of points that might be relevant in planning; and in the next section the emphasis is upon

Table 5.7

What was the single most important piece of information required about . . ., other than accumulated experience, before you took the final decision?

Response	Number of firms	Mean success rating
Whether a market existed, what was the extent of the market	9	2.6
None, other than accumulated experience	15	1.7
The nature of the competition	2	4.0
Sales performance of firm being taken over	2	3.0
Nature of, conditions of, government inducements	3	2.9
Ability of management being taken over	2	2.5
Availability and suitability of labour force	2	1.5
Ability of agent (future partner)	2	1.0
Local production specifications	1	3.0
How important it was to have a factory there	1	3.0
Whether would be welcome by local community	1	2.0
General pattern of European trade	1	1.0
What was the acceptable price for the product	1	0
Technical superiority of own product	1	0

researching the market for the product. Since the concern is with passing on the benefits of experience, it should be noted that the importance of information gathering is mentioned more often by those firms which have failed in their first overseas production subsidiary than by those firms which have been successful. Several firms attributed part of their failure to faulty or incomplete gathering of information, while ongoing success was rarely attributed to successful collection and use of information. On balance however, the experiences of the forty-three firms would suggest that the importance of information relating to the market and on operating

> **Scenario 5.4.1** Success rating: '4'
>
> A firm in the instrument and electrical engineering sector considered it crucial to investigate the products and prices of local competitors before committing financial resources to setting up a production unit in West Germany. This 'market research' was carried out by friends posing as customers of competitors. From information gathered, the firm knew that it needed to adopt different marketing strategies in its two product divisions to penetrate each market segment. Local competition in one product was strong, consequently the firm offered a better service and product at the same price as its competitors. As demand for the other product was met by imports, it was felt that the establishment of a local manufacturing unit would lead to penetration of this market segment because of the presence factor.
>
> The achievement of a sixty-seven fold increase in sales turnover in the fifteen years of operation of the overseas production subsidiary is, according to the UK chief executive, a product of successful strategy derived from information collection and evaluation.

conditions cannot be overemphasised. There appears to be no substitute for careful collection of data before the investment takes place.

Often information is both easily available and cheap. As Appendix I of this book shows, most countries provide a service to prospective investors, giving large amounts of free information on their economy, laws, aids to industry, labour conditions and costs. In addition, desk research at the local library in standard business reference books can strengthen this, and carefully planned and purposeful visits to prospective host countries are essential. In the interviews two questions sought to determine the sources of information used by the firms: 'What was the single most important *source* of information about the . . . market, other than accumulated experience, before you took the final decision?', and 'What other sources contributed to information?'. The single most important source of information for each firm is shown in Table 5.8 and subsidiary sources are shown in Table 5.9. The purpose of the two tables is simply to provide checklists of sources easily accessible to a firm considering an overseas investment. As with the sources listed in Appendix I most of these sources can be accessed without cost. The only comments on Tables 5.8 and 5.9 would be to note the nine firms which did not attempt to obtain even free information, and the twelve firms which relied on only one source of information.

Table 5.8

What was the single most important source of information about the . . . market, other than accumulated experience, before you took the final decision?

Source	Number of firms
Own experience (no information sought)	9
Potential customers	7
Banks	6
Agent	5
State agency for foreign investment	4
Acquired firm	3
Personal contacts	2
British Embassy in . . .	2
Competitors	2
Trade association	1
Supplier	1
Accountants	1
	43

To emphasise the importance of gathering information Table 5.10 shows the nature of the competition in the overseas market faced by the forty-three firms. Success is highest where the competition is from other UK firms — that is from firms whose products, methods and practices are already known

Table 5.9

What other sources contributed to information?

Source	Number of firms*
No secondary source	12
Banks in UK and . . .	4
Accountants	4
Department of Trade and Industry (UK)	4
Chamber of Commerce	3
Local planning authorities	2
Personal contacts	2
Potential customers	1
Solicitor	1

*Excludes the nine firms in Table 5.8 who did not seek information, but note that others were allowed to give more than one secondary source.

from experiences in the UK. When competition is from non-UK firms, success tends to be lower and, since most of the forty-three firms typically did not research the competitiveness of the environment they were entering, this is one obvious area where some information-gathering would pay dividends.

Table 5.10

Who are your main competitors in . . . ?

Response	Number of firms	Mean success rating
UK competitors	3	2.7
Indigenous firms	14	2.2
Other international firms	12	1.8
Other international firms plus indigenous firms	7	1.8
UK competitors plus indigenous firms	6	2.1
Not relevant	1	1.0
	43	

In summary, it must be emphasised that the costs of collecting information can be determined accurately and they are usually very low or zero, while the benefits in terms of reducing riskiness and avoiding failures can be very high. While all information carries some value to the manager in reaching a decision, a warning is in order that some sources often have a vested interest in encouraging the prospective investor to set up an overseas production subsidiary in order to increase *their own* business or ensure their own supplies. Consequently their advice should not be regarded as impartial. In terms of accurate and useful information several firms noted that commercial banks proved particularly helpful in the EEC — both UK and foreign banks being mentioned.

5.5 Market research overseas

Sales are the basic source of success and in a step-by-step decision process about the viability of an overseas production subsidiary, information on the overseas market is crucial.

However, in response to the question 'Before the first foreign investment took place, did your company become involved in market research activities in . . . ?', twenty-six of the forty-three firms replied 'No'. Thus sixty per cent of the firms sought no market information other than what they might already know from exporting there, having an agency there, or having an overseas sales subsidiary there.* In fact, and confirming Section 5.4, many firms noted that they felt they had already proved the existence of a market by their experience. A supplementary question sought to establish the kind of market research and the types are listed in Table 5.11 along with the 'No' responses.

Table 5.11 shows that five firms carried out market research consisting of visits to actual and potential customers by a manager or associate of the firm in order to introduce himself, the firm and its products, and to inform the customer of their plans to begin production in that country. This was

---

*After the first few 'No' responses, the question was usually introduced in a round-about fashion to make clear our unrestricted interpretation of market research.

Table 5.11 Market research and success

Type	Number of firms	Mean success rating
Market research consisting of visits to actual and potential customers by a manager or associate of the firm, supplemented by desk research by a manager of the firm	5	2.6
Market research consisting of visits to actual and potential customers by a manager or associate of the firm	9	2.1
No market research of any kind	26	2.0
Market research by a specialist agency	3	1.7
	43	

supplemented by some kind of desk research — determining the size of the market, the growth of the market, the growth of the economy, lists of competitors, brochures on competitors' products, competitors' prices, lists of likely customers, etc., by means of government agencies, trade associations, newspaper articles and other bodies. (It may be noted that a particularly fruitful source of overseas customers is subsidiaries or parents of UK customers, and that in many cases the UK customer is willing to contact its parent or its subsidiary overseas to give an introduction.) For these five firms the mean level of success was 2.6. This group of five has two of the 'totally successful' category and one each of 'very successful' and 'average success'; the picture is marred, however, by one in the 'failure' category, and the manager being interviewed volunteered the information that the research undertaken was 'clearly insufficient — with hindsight'.

Somewhat less extensive market research, consisting of the visits without the desk work, was carried out by nine firms with a mean success rating of 2.1.

Of the twenty-six firms, noted next in the table, it must be noted that five firms who said they carried out no market

> **Scenario 5.5.1**   Success rating: '2'
>
> Unsophisticated but, according to the chief executive of a small family firm, dominant in a market segment of the UK capital goods industry, effective market research techniques were used to test demand before the overseas production unit was established in the USA. These techniques involved firstly the identification of potential corporate customers and secondly gaining time and entry to demonstrate the product. Potential customers were identified by an ex-UK employee, US immigrant, through his acquaintanceship with a major US machine distributor. The ex-employee then carried out the basic market appraisal. In the words of the chief executive, 'despite all these modern sophisticated techniques, one still has to go out and sell'.

research activities overseas went on to attribute some of their lack of success (two were '2' and three were '0') to their lack of investigation of the market before they went ahead. One of the managers said: 'Had we sent someone to look at the market, we would not have touched it with a barge pole'. At the bottom of the list in Table 5.11 are the three firms which commissioned market research by a specialist firm. At this stage the usual rider needs to be added, to the effect that no importance can be attached to a single finding, such as the mean success of firms that commissioned outside research being lower than the firms which did other, or no, types of market research. An excellent example of this is the firm rated as '0' in the commissioned market research group: the manager noted that the appraisal of the market was extensive and correct, but they omitted to pay much attention to the abilities of their prospective partner! Each section and each chapter must be taken as part of a picture, and only the whole picture represents the true experiences of forty-three firms and their first overseas production subsidiaries.

That rider apart, it is nice to be able to note that the firms which did do the type of market research which is sensible for a small firm, did appear to be those firms which were, on average, the more successful ones. On balance, the conclusion must be that the money and executive time spent on the type of market research indicated above (visits plus desk research) is likely to be one of the best investments the small firm can make *before* it commits itself to overseas production.

5.6 Overseas visits

An overseas visit must always add some information useful to a decision, since even on a strictly non-business trip, knowledge is gained of the attitudes of public officials, taxi-drivers, waiters, and public opinion, of the climate, of the general efficiency of the country and its plumbing, of the customers and of the attitudes towards work and effort. Not surprisingly, every one of the forty-three firms had gathered some information by means of an overseas trip. The question was: 'Before the investment decision was taken, who went to . . . . . on the firm's behalf, and what did they do there?'.

A wide variety of personnel undertook these pre-investment visits, from chairmen and managing directors to engineers and technical personnel, and firms with agents or overseas sales subsidiaries in the country already often had an established pattern of visits overseas, so that information leading to the setting up of the overseas production subsidiary was collected on these general trips as well as on the special (often secret) trips.

The objects of concern in these visits were, in order of frequency mentioned: establishing the viability of the venture in terms of market size; choosing the site for the project; consultation with and evaluation of prospective partners or

> **Scenario 5.6.1** Success rating: '0'
>
> In 1960 a manufacturer of prefabricated steel and concrete industrial structures decided to expand overseas because it was making good profits in the UK. The firm had never exported because, to quote the chief executive 'transport costs kill exports stone dead'. The senior sales manager of the firm had links with France dating back to the resistance in World War II and had family ties through his French wife. The familiarity of the senior sales manager with France persuaded the chairman of the company to invest in that country. A four month market survey was carried out by the firm's own sales team. This produced market forecasts and suggested alternative locations which were later investigated by the chairman and managing director of the company. A decision was made for the chosen site, because more attractive inducements involving rebates on numbers employed, were offered by the regional and local development authorities.
>
> The managing director believes that the prospect of obtaining the free freehold of land when 200 people were employed clouded other considerations, and that the failure of the venture was a product of insufficient research, not only of the market but also of location, financing and labour considerations.

firms to acquire; meeting customers and negotiating for grants. Minor objects of interest were: conditions of employment, wage rates, availability of labour, and meetings with accountants, civil servants and lawyers. The major lesson to be learned from the experience of the firms in the sample in respect of overseas visits is that the visitors should have a clear idea of exactly what they are looking for in advance. It was pointed out to us that some visits were haphazard and ill-organised, often ending as little more than sightseeing visits. On the other hand, with more preparation, vital information was gathered and lasting impressions gained. Accordingly, it is a lesson that each visiting person should be allocated a checklist of required information and a structured search should be undertaken, otherwise the chances of getting useful knowledge are jeopardised.

In Table 5.12 the responses have been broken down into four categories as to whether one or more men went and whether one or more trips were involved.

The most extensive category is more than one man on more than one trip, and thirteen firms did this, with a mean success rating of 2.9. It is noteworthy that of the six overseas

Table 5.12

Before the investment was taken, who went to...... on the firm's behalf, and what did they do there?

	Number of firms	Mean success rating
More than one trip made by more than one man	13	2.9
More than one trip made by one man	11	2.2
One trip made by moe than one man	6	1.8
One trip made by one man	13	1.3
	43	

production subsidiaries rated as 'totally successful', five are in this category, and there were no failures. The mean for the category of more than one trip by one man is 2.2, and the success ratings are in the central range of 'very successful', 'average success' and 'not successful', the two extreme ratings being absent. The mean success rating is lower again for those firms which made one trip by more than one man before the decision was taken. The rating is 1.8 and the least extensive overseas visit, one man making one trip, was sufficient for thirteen firms, but the mean success was only 1.3 and this category had four of the total of five 'failures'. (In this category we have again the 'totally successful' investment started with £2500, which the firm was prepared to lose, and clearly wished to limit additional expense.)

While one cannot build a castle on a toadstool, Table 5.12 does give some valid information which is part of the overall picture — that the firms which did go to the trouble of exploring the country in which they then invested, have had on average more success with their overseas production subsidiaries.

Executive summary

This chapter has looked at the planning stages of an overseas production subsidiary and has considered the question of one hundred per cent versus less-than-one hundred per cent control (Section 5.1), the impact of entering the foreign market by means of takeover or greenfield venture (Section 5.2), what the firms would do differently if they were to repeat the whole operation with the benefit of hindsight (Section 5.3), the information the firms felt they required before going ahead with the decision to set up an overseas production subsidiary (Section 5.4), the kinds of market research that were carried out (Section 5.5) and in the last section, Section 5.6, the visits overseas by UK executives prior to setting up the overseas production subsidiary. Where relevant these factors were considered in relation to the success ratings of the overseas production subsidiaries established in Chapter 3.

From Section 5.1, the question of the extent of control necessary for success, on balance, probably resolves into a preference for a degree of control of seventy-five per cent or more. If the mean success ratings are a valid part of the total picture, the implication is that firms making their first overseas production subsidiary would do better to avoid ventures where their degree of control is only marginal (that is, fifty-one to seventy-four per cent) and those where they are equal or minority partners. The advantages of having local participation can be gained while control remains unchallenged by a venture in which the degree of control is seventy-five per cent or more, and this might be considered by firms about to set up their first overseas production subsidiary as an alternative to one hundred per cent control.

When the method of entry, takeover or greenfield, was considered, as in Section 5.2, the method did not appear to be a relevant factor for determining the success of the venture. This conclusion was not modified when the overseas production subsidiaries were cross-classified by method of entry and degree of control for this merely reinforced the finding in Section 5.1. What was noticeable, however, was the lack of consideration of takeover as an alternative when greenfield was expressed as the initial preference, and of greenfield when takeover was the initial preference. In principle they are alternatives and a short systematic look at one *and* the other might have been a profitable use of managerial time for many of the firms interviewed.

In Section 5.3, it was reported how firms in the survey would set up overseas production subsidiaries differently if they were to repeat the venture today. The most common response was to the effect that nothing different would be done, a response regarded as alarming given the typically low success ratings of these ventures. Any alarm apart, the purpose of the section was not to relate hindsight to success but to catalogue points learned by the forty-three firms. This section, and particularly Tables 5.5 and 5.6 could most usefully be read in conjunction with Sections 8.1 and 8.2 on 'lessons learned' and 'problems' before a decision to invest overseas is taken.

Experience accumulated in the course of business life, and in particular that gained through trading with a particular foreign country, is obviously important in a decision on an overseas production subsidiary, but the survey sought to determine what additional information was needed before the final decision on the overseas production subsidiary. In

Section 5.4 again, as commented in the previous paragraph, the importance of the findings lies in the usefulness of being able to check off what other firms have done against one's own information-collection efforts prior to investing overseas. At the risk of being pedantic, information on investing is freely and voluminously available from the government, trade associations, banks and other organisations in the country under consideration. The usefulness of the information, of course, varies but the cost of acquiring it is so low as to be negligible. Initial contacts are given in Appendix I to this book, and it would be tantamount to foolishness not to utilise these sources of free information.

Perhaps this obvious statement has to be reinforced as a result of Section 5.5 on the market research done by the firms. The most successful firms on average had contacted their existing customers to inform them of the plans for an overseas production subsidiary in their country, obtained introductions and references from UK customers to *their* parent and subsidiary companies abroad, and supplemented these sources of market information by background data easily available from UK libraries or the sources indicated in the previous paragraph. On average, the firms which did not do this type of market research were less successful.

The final section, Section 5.6, covered overseas visits by managers or associates of the UK firms prior to setting up the overseas production subsidiaries. Again, taken in isolation the data in the section are not a panacea for success, but they do suggest that success tended to go to those firms whose managers had taken the trouble to make trips to the country in which the production unit was to be sited; and in general the carefully planned trips — planned with respect to interviewing customers, banks, trade associations and ministries dealing with inward investment — were the ones associated with subsequently successful overseas production subsidiaries.

This chapter has added a few more indications of how to increase the chances of having a successful overseas production subsidiary. They will not guarantee success, of course, but they are part of the process of improving the data on which good decisions are based, and removing some risks quite unnecessarily faced by many small firms.

6 The investing stages

The factors which remain to be considered are the product-price-marketing decision, the objectives set for the venture, the siting of the factory, inducements offered by the host government, and exchange control permission from the Bank of England. Ideally these factors would be considered and decisions made before the first turf was turned or the first share purchased; but as indicated at the start of Chapter 5, the process of setting up an overseas production subsidiary was, for many of the firms, not a step-by-step evaluation and decision process, but a muddled process. Perhaps the best examples relevant to this chapter are the three firms who invested abroad without even knowing that they needed Bank of England permission to do so!

The first section of this chapter looks at the segment of the market in the host country at which the overseas production subsidiary aimed its product; in Section 6.2 that market attack is compared with that in the UK; Section 6.2 also looks at how the firm chose which product, or products, to manufacture in its new overseas production unit and how this production was developed. After these general product-price-marketing decisions, attention is turned to the objectives set by the firms for their overseas production subsidiaries, and in particular the financial objectives which were set (Section 6.3). Section

6.4 looks at the prime factor considered by the firm in selecting the actual site for the production unit, and Section 6.5 looks at inducements offered by the host government and which ones were taken up by the firms in this survey. The final section, Section 6.6, examines the firms' experiences in obtaining exchange control permission from the Bank of England. As in previous chapters, there are some indications, particularly in the product-price-marketing discussion, of a relationship between the decisions made and the success of the overseas production subsidiary, which are probably a relevant feature of the overall relationship with success.

6.1 Marketing and pricing strategy

Sales are the source of income to the firm and sales are generated by having the right product at the right price in the right market at the right time. In this section the concern is with the price and the market. (The product is examined in the next section.) Price and market are usually combined so that the overall strategy is to sell to one segment of the market, say the quality end of the range, and the price is adjusted accordingly. Equally, the choice might be to go for the mass market end of the range, or the part of the market where price is the major element in the purchaser's decision, and price is again influenced by this strategy.

The first task in this respect is therefore to determine at what level of the market in the foreign country the forty-three survey firms aimed for. The question was: 'Given that you have competitors in . . . , at what level of the consumer market do you orientate your sales promotion activities: (1) high price, 'luxury' end of market; (2) medium price, middle market range; (3) low price, mass market range?'. The responses are in Table 6.1. The first point to note is that eleven firms did not regard the question as applicable, generally because they were in some type of contract market where they supplied a specialised product to a customer's specifications. The question was relevant to thirty-two firms, and of these twenty-one aimed at the top end of the market.

Table 6.1

Given that you have competitors in . . ., at what level of the market do you orientate your sales promotion activities?

Response	Number of firms	Mean success rating
High price, 'luxury' end of market	21	2.3
Medium price, middle market range	3	1.0
Low price, mass market range	5	2.0
Multi-price strategy	3	1.7
Not applicable	11	
	43	

These twenty-one firms covered all levels of success and the mean success rating is 2.3. The middle market was the target for three firms, the low end of the market was the target for five firms, and three firms aimed at all segments by varying price and quality appropriately. While the mean success for middle market range firms is low at 1.0, the mean for the mass market firms is 2.0, only slightly less than the mean of firms aiming for the top end of the market. The closeness of the means suggests that there is no strong relationship between market segmentation and success. There is a indication however that the multi-strategy and middle range firms in fact had no clear strategy. This is perhaps the best explanation of these groups' relative failures.

It may be worthwhile, however, for a firm contemplating setting up an overseas production subsidiary to consider going for the top end of the market — as the majority of the firms in the sample did, because in the first place an overseas production subsidiary often faces higher costs than its local competitors — costs of operating at a distance from the parent and costs arising from inadequate knowledge of local conditions. This is particularly true in the early life of the overseas production subsidiary, and these higher costs are

> **Scenario 6.1.1** Success rating: '3'
>
> A firm established in the nineteenth century purchased a firm in Australia in 1948 to serve better the Australian market and to be ready for the growth they believed Australia would experience. They kept on the owner as the new chief executive but fired him after eighteen months as he could not adjust to working for someone else. Over time the UK products were introduced to the Australian firm and the personnel were trained as the changes were made, so that after a few years the Australian products were, as the UK products, 'high quality-top end of the market — we just don't know the needs of the mass market, it is not our business'.

more easily absorbed with a high-priced quality product. Second, returns in the top end of the market can be earned from a lower volume of production, which could be crucial in the early months (even years) of the life of the overseas production subsidiary. This advice must be constrained however by the findings in the next paragraphs.

As the next step in the analysis, the firms have been categorised according to whether their foreign market segment target was the same as that in the UK, or whether they had decided in going to the foreign country to change their marketing strategy. The results are in Table 6.2. Twenty-six firms stayed with the marketing strategy they knew and did not change for the host country market. All levels of success were achieved and the mean success rating was 2.3. There were six firms which did change their marketing strategy, and the highest level of success achieved was 'average' and there were three failures. The mean success rating was 0.8.

The customary warning is in order: here is one isolated observation and placing too much reliance upon it is dangerous; however, it may be a valid piece of the overall relationship with success. With that warning, the impression from Table 6.2 is that the firms which do stay with their proven marketing strategy achieve the normal range of success

Table 6.2

Did you orientate your sales promotion activities in . . . to the same level of market as in the UK?

Response	Number of firms	Mean success rating
Foreign sales promotion, pricing, etc. same as UK	26	2.3
Foreign sales promotion, pricing, etc. not same as UK	6	0.8
Not applicable	11	
	43	

expected from firms making their first overseas production subsidiary, while the firms who do not stay with the marketing strategy with which they are familiar may be more likely to meet with a lack of success or even outright failure.

In fact all the six firms which did change their marketing strategy did so in a downwards direction, that is moving from the higher quality, less price conscious top end of the market toward the lower quality, price sensitive lower end of the market. Their reasoning, while it has some appeal — it was that they would have to compete with the local firms on their terms — has its obvious dangers in that the local firms know their market and the new UK unit does not, and further the strategy is not attempting to utilise the firm's UK marketing expertise or build on its export sales which were directed to the same marketing segment as in the UK. The hypothesis that failure is more likely to be associated with a novel marketing strategy seems a reasonable one and the lesson follows that firms setting up their first overseas production subsidiary should pursue their UK marketing strategy in terms of quality, price and promotion.

> **Scenario 6.1.2** Success rating: '0'
>
> Within the general heating and ventilation field in the UK the firm produced a specialised product which on a price or a running cost basis was not competitive except in specialised applications. The firm is successful in the UK. It opened a small factory in Holland and priced its product to compete directly with the other products which have wide applications in the heating and ventilation market. 'We are definitely up-market in the UK; it is what we should have been in Holland; we wouldn't dream of competing with . . . in the UK so why did we in Holland? I suppose because the factory was only half occupied and we thought if we cut prices we would increase the volume . . .'

6.2 Product policy and the development of production

A key part of the overall product price strategy is the choice of product. The firm could choose to manufacture in its first overseas production unit the full range of products manufactured in the UK, a selected part of that range, one product from that range, or a product not manufactured in the UK. Accordingly one question was directed to this choice: 'At that time, how did you decide which of your products to product in the . . . plant?'. The basis for the decisions are shown in Table 6.3.

The most common way the firms decided which product(s) to manufacture overseas was by analysing their exports to the country in which the overseas production unit was to be sited. Of the forty-three firms, twenty-five decided this way. As Table 6.3 shows, this includes firms which were basically one-product companies. These one-product companies were relatively successful in their first overseas production venture. The lowest rating was 'average success' and basically this accords with the general hypothesis that if a firm stays with its successful product — which it is successfully exporting — then it is more likely to be successful with manufacturing it overseas for that market. Of course, the firm could come unstuck on the manufacturing side if it tried to produce overseas by methods different from those employed in the UK, but this

Table 6.3

At that time, how did you decide which of your products to produce in the . . . plant?

Response	Number of firms	Mean success rating
Analysed own exports to that country and chose:		
(i) product(s) with highest sales	13	2.5
(ii) product(s) with simplest manufacturing processes	3	2.3
(iii) product(s) with lowest value/weight	2	2.5
(iv) product(s) with lowest capital requirement	1	4.0
(v) product(s) with highest profit	2	2.5
(vi) product(s) with highest labour content	1	1.0
Only one UK product	3	3.0
All export-based decisions	25	2.6
Continued products in company taken over	3	1.3
All UK products	6	0.8
Based on a general look at the market there	1	0
Market pointed out to us	1	4.0
Least competition in this product	1	3.0
Shortage of capacity in UK	1	2.0
The product not already exported there	1	2.0
Completely new product	1	2.0
Recommended by agents	1	1.0
Specific market research	1	0
Not applicable	1	2.0
	43	

section is concerned with marketing, and staying with an established marketing procedure, rather than trying a new one, will probably reduce one area of risk.

Returning to the twenty-two firms which manufactured more than one product in the UK, thirteen of these chose to manufacture the product, or the small range of products, which had the highest sales in the market in which the overseas production subsidiary was to be set up. The mean success rating for these firms, at 2.5, reflects the presence in this group of three of the six 'totally successful' overseas production subsidiaries and the absence of 'failures'. Three other firms among the twenty-two chose the products with the simplest manufacturing processes. This is again risk-reduction in practice, since *a priori* there are fewer opportunities for mistakes if the manufacturing process is simple. A further two firms chose to manufacture in the overseas production subsidiary those export products which had the lowest value/weight ratio. Thus while the firms had proved they could profitably export such products from the UK to the foreign market, the decision was that higher profits could be earned if the handling and transportation costs, which were high relative to the total invoice value, were avoided by local manufacture. In a similar fashion the remaining four firms chose the product(s) which needed the lowest amount of capital investment to manufacture (risk-reduction in respect of capital committed), which had the highest rate of profit (risk-reduction in that the profit could more easily absorb unanticipated costs), and which had the highest labour content (to match the low-wage labour available in the host country). Overall this group of twenty-five firms, as can be seen from Table 6.3, were relatively successful: five of the six 'totally successful' firms are among the twenty-five (thus eighty-three per cent of the totally successful firms are in fifty-eight per cent of the sample) and there is an absence of 'failures'.

Another way of arriving at the decision as to which product(s) to manufacture overseas is simply to continue the products in the firm taken over. Of the three firms continuing

> **Scenario 6.2.1 Success rating: '1'**
>
> A basically similar product was sold by the firm to two fairly distinct markets — domestic and contract — and there was a pricing and marketing policy for each. The firm bought a struggling factory in South Africa at a time when the firm's exports to both product markets had been growing fast, but one was eighty per cent of exports, the other twenty per cent. The distributors in South Africa advised the firm to make a big push for the product market which on export figures was the smaller (that is, the twenty per cent). 'The accountant in the UK worked on paper and passed the policy on paper, but there was no business sense in the decision — we didn't do our homework and we tried to expand the wrong area.'

to produce the products of the firm they acquired, the success ratings are one '3' and two '1's. Again expressing caution as to the significance of single cause-effect observations, the firm with the '3' did follow a policy of gradual but definite substitution of its own products for those already manufactured by the newly acquired subsidiary, while the firms with the '1' rating continued wholly to manufacture the existing products.

Six firms avoided the selection problem by choosing to produce overseas all the products currently manufactured in the UK. It would appear that this is not a successful policy, perhaps because of the greater task it implies, for the best rating is only 'average success' and out of a total of five failures among the forty-three firms, three were in this category.

The balance of the forty-three firms, those not explicitly covered by the comments above, are listed in Table 6.3 and will be of interest to other firms whose decision has been based, or is about to be based, on one of the criteria shown.

In addition to the decision on which product(s), the scale of production has to be decided and consequently the firms were asked if they had entered the market at too small a scale. Five firms said that they did so deliberately with a view to minimising risk and capital outlay — oddly, one of these firms later overcommitted itself by undertaking an over-ambitious expansion! — and one felt that it had in fact entered the market on too large a scale. The remainder of the firms (except three of the 'failures' who felt that they should never have entered at all) said that their scale of entry was about right and that later expansion after entry resulted from increased market penetration. There is a natural reticence to commit capital initially to an overseas production subsidiary, but the balancing problem is that of over optimism on the part of agents and partners. The smaller firms are, of course, severely limited by the quantity of capital which they can raise, particularly in the initial stages of the venture. (Exchange control regulations also require capital outlays to be kept to a minimum.) The problem is one of uncertainty, for which the only counter strategy is to amass as much *reliable* information as possible on market size and market trends as well as full internal appraisal of the capability and commitment of supporting an optimum-sized overseas production subsidiary. On this basis more confidence can be placed in the ability of the overseas production subsidiary to exploit the market fully. In many cases flexibility was built into the overseas project, by such means as renting premises or choosing a site where expansion could be easy and cheap. If possible such degrees of freedom in size should be built in to the project, at least in the early stages.

This section has looked at the product-market decision and the results are in uniformity with the emerging portrait of the successful overseas production subsidiary. Success tended to go to those firms whose product-market decisions were based upon their existing expertise — in short they duplicated overseas their strategies, prices and products proven in the UK and in exporting. Departures from these resulted often in the lower levels of success and in failure.

6.3 Performance objectives

Textbooks are categoric that objectives be set for any venture. The objectives are a starting point for the analysis of the investment and criteria by which the venture would be judged. Thus an objective might be set in terms of a share of the market in the foreign country and this implies a certain volume of sales; and on the basis of the selling prices of existing exports it follows that there is some basic flow of cash implied by the market share. This flow into the overseas production subsidiary might then be compared with the cash expenditure (such as wages, materials purchases and marketing costs) necessary to sustain that level of sales, and a comparison of the two cash flows would enable some assessment of the profitability of the venture to be made. The UK firm would have set some target rate of profitability — which would allow a decision on the exercise just completed. These exercises serve two purposes. One is that (hopefully) a better decision will result; the second lies in the discipline implied by the exercise itself — it forces senior managers to think about the basic factors (the level of sales and the level of costs) and this in turn may feed back into making the decision a better one.

In Section 3.2 the idea was put forward that an overseas investment is a venture subject to more risk than a venture in the UK because of the problems of operating in a relatively less well-known environment and of operating at a distance. Following that idea, an overseas venture should be subject to more analysis and more searching questioning than a project in the UK, and this should be reflected in the objectives set for the venture.

Accordingly, one question asked: 'Before you commenced

production in . . . , what objectives did you set for the overseas subsidiary in terms of performance?'. Just about a quarter of the firms (ten out of forty-three) said they had set no objectives! Their success ratings are shown in Table 6.4. In spite of having set no objectives, two of the ten firms were rated as 'totally successful'. One was the venture started with an investment of £2500 and since the firm regarded this as a straight win or loss gamble, perhaps there was no need for objectives to be set. The other was also a fairly small

Table 6.4

Before you commenced production in . . ., what objectives did you set for the overseas subsidiary in terms of performance?

Objectives	Number of firms	Mean success rating
Production	6	1.2
Pay-back period	5	1.6
Self-financing	2	2.0
Market share	4	2.3
Return on investment	4	2.8
Profit level	4	2.8
Multiple	8	2.8
All objectives	33	2.2
All multiple objectives	16	2.8
All single objectives	17	1.6
No objectives	10	1.6

investment, £10 000, and since turnover in the first year was only DM23 000, again the position might be viewed more as a gamble than an investment. While these are the two firms rated as '4' and they invested little, the other firms which did not set objectives did invest typically larger sums and met with less than total success. One firm rated '0' invested 15 million Belgian francs and the overseas production subsidiary just about broke even for the first four years, then began to turn in heavy losses.

The other thirty-three firms did set some performance

objectives for their proposed venture into overseas manufacturing. Some firms set multiple objectives, much as is implied in the first paragraph of this section. Eight firms set such multiple objectives, and the mean success rating is 2.8, as shown in Table 6.4. Again, there are two firms rated as 'totally successful'. One of these set targets in respect of market share, net return on sales and net return on capital employed. The overseas production subsidiary met the targets in its first year. Other than these eight firms, the remaining twenty-five set a single objective for their first production venture abroad. Common ones were a level of profit to be achieved in the first or subsequent years, a break-even position to be achieved within a time target, a share of the market in that country within a time target and a stated return on the amount invested by the UK firm; in two cases the objective was that the overseas production subsidiary was to be self-financing after the initial capital transfer, that is, it could not look to the UK parent for further funds. The eight firms which set multiple objectives had a mean success rating of 2.8, as noted above, and this mean rating was matched by another eight firms, four of which set a return on investment objective and four a profit-level objective. While these latter two are single objectives, they are objectives which require multiple estimates — for example, they both need revenue and cost data to support the objectives. These can be contrasted with the truly single objectives — production level (six firms), pay-back period (five firms), self-financing (two firms) and market share (four firms) — which require only a single piece of data. These seventeen firms averaged a success rating of 1.6, identical to the firms which set no objectives.

Thus in terms of rankings that result from the analysis of Table 6.4, as an overall average the firms with objectives for their overseas venture did better than firms with no objectives but the highest average success went to the firms with multiple objectives for their overseas venture and the firms with single objectives fared no differently on average from the firms with no objectives. On balance, common business sense must prevail in the longer term and success will go to those firms which take the time and the care to set objectives and to assess ventures against the firm's chosen objectives.

From overall objectives (if any) the questioning turned to purely financial objectives: 'Looking purely at financial objectives, were your targets set in any of the following ways: rate of return on book assets, positive cash flow after . . . years, discounted cash flow analysis, or some other way?'. The most common response, in line with the previous question, was that no financial objectives had been set for the venture. Thus, over half of the firms (twenty-five out of forty-three) had invested money overseas without setting financial objectives for the investment. Of the ones which did set objectives, the preference was for a target rate of return on book assets. The average success rating for these firms was 2.9, one of the highest averages occurring in any table. Eleven firms set such an objective, and seven set an objective of a positive cash flow after a given period of time — in other words, the overseas production subsidiary would be allowed to take cash away from the UK firm for a given period of time, after which the overseas production subsidiary would be expected to make profits. No firms used a discounted cash flow method of analysis even though *The Economist* as long ago as 1966 assumed everyone knew about discounted cash flow techniques.* The question asked in the interviews was open-ended to catch any other financial objectives but, as noted in Table 6.5, there were no financial objectives other than rate of return and positive cash flow.

Again it would appear that the observations accord in general with common business sense in that the firms which did set financial objectives appeared to be more successful in their first foreign production investment.

The final piece of analysis in this section on the objectives set for the overseas venture concerns the responses to the question: 'In terms of financial targets, were you expecting a

---

* *The Economist*, 15 January 1966, page 201.

Table 6.5

Looking purely at financial objectives, were your targets set in any of the following ways?

Objectives	Number of firms	Mean success rating
Rate of return on book assets	11	2.9
Positive cash flow after x years	7	1.9
Discounted cash flow analysis	0	0
Other	0	0
All financial objectives	18	2.5
No financial objectives	25	1.8

higher return on your overseas investment than you expect on your UK investments?'. Again the reasoning concerns risk. The overseas venture is subject to more risk and conventional financial theory says that an additional premium in terms of rate of return is required where there is additional risk. In Table 6.6, however, only seven firms out of the forty-three were looking for compensation for the extra risk of investing overseas; and these are the same firms which have set multiple objectives and financial objectives in the two earlier tables in this section. Their extra awareness appears to have paid off in that the mean success rating for these firms is 2.6, compared with 2.0 for the remaining firms.

The hypothesis underlying this section is trite: it is that those firms which set objectives appropriate to an overseas investment were on average more successful. It is trite because setting objectives is a recognised part of the professional

Table 6.6

In terms of financial targets, were you expecting a higher rate of return on your overseas investment than you expect on your UK investments?

Response	Number of firms	Mean success rating
Yes	7	2.6
No	36	2.0

management function. The collection of data to formulate and set objectives and to compare performance with objectives is a method of improving the quality of a decision. At its simplest all this section has shown is that the firms which did the work implied by setting objectives were those firms with the more successful overseas production subsidiaries. Perhaps, the section has shown something even more simple: since setting objectives is a recognised part of professional management, the results show the firms with professional management are the more successful. However simple, the lesson is clear, and consistent with other sections, success tends to go to those firms which work toward it.

6.4 Selection of the production site

If the location of the site is not chosen carefully, the overseas production subsidiary will be bearing costs greater than its local competitors. The subsidiary could be hauling supplies further than its competitors, or shipping its finished goods further, or paying higher rents or labour charges because it is a high-cost locality.

The selection of the site can be made for a variety of reasons, and a question was designed to elicit the reasoning used by the forty-three firms in the survey: 'What was the single most important factor in choosing . . . as the site for the firm's production unit?'.

Table 6.7 shows that the most common reason was that the export agent, licensee or distributor was already located there, and of course in the case of takeovers the site was selected by the choice of firm taken over. Twenty firms sited their production unit because of this pre-selection factor. They cover all the range of success and the mean rating is 2.0, exactly 'average success'. This method is not of course akin to a random location of the unit, because presumably the agent, licensee, distributor or existing firm are located where they are for reasons which will include economic factors.

However, even though the site in these cases was pre-selected on the basis of some reasons which include economic ones, it is possible that the UK firm which was *fully* able to select the site may be better placed. (For example, economic conditions may have changed since the existing locations were chosen by agents, etc.) UK firms in this position would typically be ones with a greenfield venture in which the local partner did not have land or a factory standing idle awaiting a use. For these firms a variety of reasons were advanced for the site selection.

Table 6.7

What was the single most important factor in choosing . . . as the site for the firm's production unit?

Response	Number of firms	Mean success rating
Closest to the largest market	3	3.0
Supplies of labour	5	2.4
Supplies of inputs other than labour	5	2.4
Low cost of land and buildings	3	2.3
Our industry is concentrated there	2	2.0
All economic factors	18	2.4
Agent, distributor or acquired firm already there	20	2.0
For ease of communications to UK	4	1.3
To have product associated with other quality products made in that location	1	2.0

They are listed in Table 6.7 and include siting the unit close to the largest market for the product, labour availability, low cost land and buildings, and close to supplies of raw materials. The success ratings for each are also shown in Table 6.7, but given the small number of firms putting forward each reason, it may be better to concentrate on these firms as a whole — shown as 'all economic factors' in the table. While the group of firms numbers eighteen — and this is less than half of the total sample — five of the six 'totally successful' ventures are in this group. This, together with the fact that the group has proportionately fewer outcomes at the lower levels of success, boosts the mean success rating to 2.4.

It will also be seen from Table 6.7 that the four firms which sited their production unit for ease of access to the UK (that is, to minimise UK management's travelling time) did not have successful overseas subsidiaries.

The empirical evidence in Table 6.7 is not sufficient to be conclusive but again it conforms to some notion of common business sense; that firms which select the site for production for some economic reason may have more success than firms in which the choice of agent or other new partner predetermines the site.

Scenario 6.4.1   Success rating: '4'

The small firm specialising in one part of the electronics field highlighted in Scenario 4.3.2 provides a useful example of the choosing of a site of its West German operation. In 1970 the firm bought out a marketing operation in Cologne, and asked the British manager to find his own successor. The first task of the new chief executive (a local national) was to move the entire operation to Frankfurt, the centre of the West German electronics industry, although the UK firm believes that the decision was partly emotional because the chief executive wanted to live in that area. When the go-ahead for a production unit was given, an empty shell (an old leather goods factory) was acquired because of its proximity to a large pool of trained labour, which the firm could bid for, in the nearby factories of one of Europe's largest electrical goods manufacturers.

6.5 Host country inducements

Many countries offer inducements to firms to set up production units within their borders. The inducements may come from the central government of the country or from some regional or local government body and in fact, there are few countries where the inducements apply equally to all locations within the country. It is more common for the inducements to depend upon the region or locality in which the production unit is established, and/or to depend upon the type of production to be carried out (with labour intensive production normally attracting the highest levels of inducements). Appendix I to this book gives a summary of inducements country by country.

Inducements can be an important aid to profitability, and the question was asked: 'Before you took your final decision to invest in . . . , did you investigate any inducements offered by the . . . government?'. Table 6.8 shows that twenty-eight firms did investigate the availability of inducements, but fifteen did not. The mean success rating is slightly higher for those which

Table 6.8

Before you took your final decision to invest in . . ., did you investigate any inducements offered by the . . . government?

Response	Number of firms	Mean success rating
Yes	28	2.2
No	15	1.8
	43	

did seek inducements, which is again consistent with the emerging picture that the firms which investigated and planned were the ones which were, on average, more successful.

The follow up question was: 'What inducements did you take up?'. In fact twenty-nine took up no inducements, the number being made up of the fifteen who did not investigate the possibility and a further fourteen who found either they were not eligible (wrong location, not large enough, not labour intensive enough), the inducements were insufficient to make them locate in the 'development area', or, (in one case) not worth the trouble of going through the bureaucracy.

It appeared in the survey that availability of labour is one of the crucial variables in the siting decision, but it was important that labour should be of the right type, having the appropriate skills. At least three firms turned down financial assistance because the right type of labour was not available. To quote one chief executive: 'We cannot afford to go to these less developed areas with our type of product. We need labour which has skill, technical competence and capability.' The remaining fourteen firms did take up inducements. The average success rating for the firms which did not take up inducements is slightly higher than those which did; perhaps this is an indication of the fact that inducements are only offered by host governments when there is a problem to overcome (remoteness, lack of infrastructure, poorly trained labour, etc.) and the inducements are barely sufficient to overcome the problem. The inducements which were taken up by the fourteen firms in the survey are listed in Table 6.9. The

Table 6.9

What inducements did you take up? Response	Number of firms	Mean success rating
None	29	2.2
Long-term loans at less than market rate of interest	6	
Cash grants on plant and equipment	5	
Tax rebate on export earnings	3	
Other tax inducements	2	
Rebates on training, or number employed	4	
Low-cost factory	2	
All inducements	14	1.9

* Column sums to more than fourteen as more than one inducement was taken up by some firms.

most common — and from the interviews the one which was the most welcome and useful — was long-term finance available at less than the going rate of interest.

One conclusion of this section is that firms which do investigate inducements tend to be slightly more successful, which is perhaps only a reflection of the fact these firms were the ones in which more care was taken in setting up the first overseas production subsidiary. Another conclusion is that firms which actually take up inducements tend to be slightly less successful, maybe suggesting that inducements themselves are insufficient to compensate for the problems that cause

---

Scenario 6.5.1 Success rating: '2'

A Yorkshire based firm of precision engineers set up a manufacturing unit for a new product in Ireland in 1960. Ireland was chosen as the host country of the investment because of the financial inducement which exempted exports from profits tax for fifteen years. The firm services UK and European demand for the product from the Irish unit, which exports its entire output. As the chief executive says: 'When you take a fifty-two per cent rate of tax on profits over fifteen years, it adds up to a lot'.

In addition the initial investment qualified for a capital expenditure grant amounting to sixty per cent of the investment outlay and grants were obtained to subsidise the costs of labour training. Later expansions have also met the criteria laid down for financial assistance and the firm has received cash grants totalling fifty-five per cent and forty per cent of investment expenditure for its two Irish expansions. Inducements are, to quote the firm, 'fairly essential because otherwise we could not afford to go ahead with the investment plans'.

inducements to be offered by host governments in the first place. Finally, a point can be made to host governments: there was a strong feeling in the survey that low-cost loans are the most appreciated inducement to investment.

6.6 Exchange control

All outward investment by UK firms requires Bank of England permission for exchange control purposes. The authorities concern themselves with the method of financing investment and, with some exceptions, will only allow the firm to purchase foreign exchange at the official rate for investment purposes if the returns to the UK will exceed the investment outlay in the short run — that is, if the investment is deemed a super-criterion project (see Appendix II). All other investments have to be financed through the investment currency market, back-to-back loans, or the free transfer of exports. While Appendix II gives details of exchange control permission, this section reports upon the firms' experiences with the Bank of England. Contact with the Bank of England is a necessary part of the overseas investment decision, as approval of financing intentions is mandatory.

In fact sixteen firms received permission to invest overseas without conditions being imposed — these were all investors in the Overseas Sterling Area or Scheduled Territories (at the time of these investments capital transfers to these areas were unrestricted, which is no longer the case). Table 6.10 shows the time taken to complete the negotiations process for the twenty-seven firms where conditions were imposed. In only one case was investment permission given after *more* than six months. It will be noted from Table 6.10 that three firms did not seek permission to transfer capital for investment purposes, and the Bank of England eventually discovered the fact. All three firms had to apply for permission retrospectively and to use the words of one manager, the man from the Bank of England was 'cross'; but none of the three firms was involved in any legal or other sanctions because of their failure to obtain permission before transferring capital — of course that does not mean that other transgressors will be treated leniently!

In terms of relations with the Bank, nine firms commented upon the difficulties they had had, or were having with the Bank. In some cases this appeared to be nothing more than a

Table 6.10 Exchange control permission

Response	Number of firms
1. No exchange control conditions imposed	16
2. Exchange control permission under stipulated conditions. Time taken for permission to be granted:	27
3 months or less	15
4-6 months	5
6 months or more	1
Permission not sought!	3
Not known	3
	43

lack of cordial relationships between people with different objectives, but in other cases the difficulties were very real. Of particular concern was the apparent latitude given to Bank officials to set the terms of the transfer. This arises because of changes in the attendant conditions of exchange control in different time periods, and misunderstandings of the Bank's current criteria (see Appendix II). It is worthwhile for managers to maintain up-to-date knowledge of current exchange control practices. Thus in one case the transfer was allowed without payment of the dollar premium, while in another the firm had to pay the premium on every capital transfer, even minimal ones. In some cases conditions were attached (such as specifying the percentage of profits to be remitted to the UK), while in others no conditions were attached. The problems arise, of course, when managers talk to each other and find that they have been treated in what they perceive to be an arbitrary fashion. One specific problem which occurred several times was the insistence by the Bank on profits forecasts for the venture, when of course, as shown in Section 6.3, many firms do not invest that way. And finally, it does appear that the Bank is more strict and more probing when a second capital transfer is requested. This is acutely so in respect of a second capital transfer to an existing venture, but also in respect of a first transfer for a second overseas venture. Equally the Bank appears less strict when the financing of any venture will be by means of a back-to-back loan* rather than a transfer of funds from the UK.

Scenario 6.6.1   Success rating: '3'

The firm, based in North-West England, decided in 1962 to produce in West Germany, at the request of its major customer (who had in fact introduced the product to them). The production process was simple and the capital requirement was DM20 000 (then about £6000). After the initial problems, the profit built up and the firm has remitted the seventy per cent of profits required by the Bank of England. Over the last few years the money *remitted* to the UK has averaged around £20 000 per year, and the firm was intensely annoyed this year when the Bank required it to pay the investment premium when it wished to expand the factory.

The lesson from the experiences of the twenty-seven firms investing outside the Sterling Area which have had contact with the Bank of England is for the firm approaching the Bank to prepare its case well before it makes its first approach. The sections in each chapter give clear indications of relevant

---

*A back-to-back loan is one where funds are borrowed locally in, say, Belgium, but guaranteed by a deposit at a UK bank. (The firm of course runs a continuing exchange risk on this type of financing.)

determinants of a successful overseas venture and basically the Bank is looking for ventures which over time will make a positive contribution to the UK foreign reserves. Two visits to the Bank appear to be normal, the second to clarify points raised in the first visit, but a well reasoned, well prepared venture will get exchange control permission with a minimum of problems and a minimum of conditions attached. As one manager said, it is a question of getting the balance between reality and the appearance of perfection!

Executive summary

This chapter has shown the need for careful consideration at the investing stages of setting up an overseas production subsidiary.

In Section 6.1 the product-price-market decisions of investing firms were examined, and although no clear relationship emerged between market segmentation strategy and success, there may be sound economic reasons for foreign market entrants to direct their products to the top-end of the host market in terms of price and quality. The reasoning is couched in terms of the higher costs associated with operating at a distance and unfamiliarity with local customs and business practices *vis-à-vis* indigenous manufacturers, which can be absorbed more readily in higher prices at lower break-even levels of output. In the same section, a clear result of analysing the success of the forty-three firms was that investing firms should stick to their UK quality, price and promotion strategy because it is in this area that they can transfer knowledge and expertise to the host country market. Indeed the firms which changed their marketing strategy to compete in an unfamiliar market environment were, on average, much less successful than those firms which attacked parallel markets.

In Section 6.2 it was shown that twenty-four firms based the choice of product for local manufacture on export-based decisions and that these selective market-based product decisions were more successful than attempts to produce the entire UK product range or to continue with an acquired firm's products. The latter may be sensible if the reason for takeover is to acquire technology and patents, but this was not the case for any of the sample firms. The most successful takeovers were those which brought into local manufacture UK products chosen on the basis of market-orientated decisions.

In Section 6.3 the setting of performance objectives for the overseas production subsidiary was examined. On average, multiple, market-orientated objectives rather than single objectives appeared to lead to more successful overseas production subsidiaries. This probably reflects the greater planning that is necessary with multiple objectives. The section also looked at financial targets and throughout the book the need of achieving a higher rate of return overseas than in the UK to compensate for greater risks of operating in an alien environment is stressed. It is important because unless greater returns are achieved, the firm would have been better off by investing in the UK, where it has intimate knowledge of local conditions. The targets set for the performance of the overseas production subsidiary emerged from investment appraisal based on information and data gathered and evaluated in the planning stages and again these were on average the more successful firms.

Section 6.4 showed that for almost half the sample the location of the overseas production subsidiary was predetermined, reflecting acceptance of the location of the existing agent, distributor, or acquired firm's plant. This may be appropriate because of the many factors which have to be considered in siting a production unit, and until the firm familiarises itself with the host market environment it will not be aware of its optimal location — the cost of imperfect location are outweighed by the benefits of operating initially in known conditions. Three firms which had the initial site chosen for them have since moved the subsidiary, and two others are contemplating doing so. For the firms with a free choice as to location success tended to go to those firms which emphasised economic factors in the location decision (such as nearness to market, labour, etc.) rather than, for example, a factor such as convenience of visits from the UK.

When inducements are analysed (the concern of Section 6.5) the first point to remember is that inducements are offered to offset the disadvantages of operating in the area. With this in mind, the firms which did investigate the inducements were on average slightly more successful than those that did not; but the firms which actually took up inducements (as opposed to merely investigating them) were slightly less successful. There is no paradox; the probable reason is that the firms which carried out investigations are those which generally learned and prepared more carefully and those which did take up inducements may have found the inducements to be insufficient compensation for operating at that location. Nevertheless for some firms, in some industries regional development assistance can be a useful source of finance, which should be taken into account in the location decision. Indeed as the level and availability of regional development assistance increases, examination of inducements is essential. One firm recommends a policy of 'grantsmanship' which involves shopping around the alternative host country authorities for inducements before the location of the overseas production subsidiary is decided.

The chapter was concluded by discussing in Section 6.6 the need to obtain, and the conditions attached to, the granting of exchange control permission. Exchange control policy is stated to be protective of the UK balance of payments and is not intended to prevent overseas investment. Firms which had visited the Bank of England to discuss their proposed overseas investment were generally granted permission in a shorter time period. These firms also had the best relationship with the Bank, although most firms described their relations with the Bank of England as cordial. Good relations also facilitated the approach to the Bank for further overseas investments. Some firms had unhappy relationships with the Bank and the problems that can be caused by the Bank make a carefully prepared approach to the Bank essential.

As with the previous chapter, this chapter has shown that success in setting up an overseas production subsidiary is earned by good management rather than it being the outcome of chance.

7 Controlling the subsidiary

Managing at a distance for the first time brings new problems for the firm. Thus while the last three chapters have concentrated on the establishment of a successful overseas production subsidiary, this chapter puts the emphasis upon methods of ensuring continuing operational success. Consequently control procedures will be related to success, for in the absence of data or experience the choice between allowing the overseas production subsidiary a great deal of autonomy (which has the risk of local management ruining the venture) and strict control (which may stifle all enterprise in the overseas unit) is a very difficult one to make.

This chapter proceeds as follows: Section 7.1 examines financial control and the overseas production subsidiary by means of accounts, budget estimates and capital expenditure authorisation; Section 7.2 analyses control of the various functions while Section 7.3 compares such control with that of UK subsidiaries; Section 7.4 looks at the contentious question of the choice of chief executive; and Section 7.5 examines the additional financial problems of reinvestment and transfer pricing. The final section looks at the trade flows between the firm and its overseas production subsidiary. As usual, an executive summary concludes the chapter.

7.1 Financial control

An indication of where responsibility for decision-making lies can be obtained from the extent of the financial information flow from the overseas production subsidiary to its parent. If UK management is to make effective decisions there is an absolute need for head office to be well informed financially, otherwise capital, management time and other valuable resources can be squandered. Accordingly the question was asked: 'How often does your overseas subsidiary submit budget estimates and accounts to the UK in the current year?'.

Table 7.1 shows an analysis of the responses to that question and the first point to note is that the table in fact shows responses to the submission of accounts. Only seven firms were

Table 7.1

How often does your overseas subsidiary submit accounts to the UK in the current year?

Response	Number of firms	Mean success rating
Never	2	1.0
Rarely	3	1.0
All accounting done in UK	5	1.6
Annually, semi-annually or quarterly	13	1.8
Monthly	20	2.6
	43	

currently using budget estimates (see below). Perhaps the most surprising point in Table 7.1 is that in two cases accounts are never submitted. Apart from the question of how the UK firms consolidate their accounts without accounts from their subsidiaries, it was obvious that control in these subsidiaries was nearly zero, and Table 7.1 shows the mean success rating to be 1.0. A mean success rating of 1.0 was also achieved in the three cases where the response was 'rarely'. Again, without necessarily reaching strong conclusions on the basis of particular pieces of data, it would appear that where control (in the form of accounts) is absent, or nearly so, that only a low success level will be achieved by the overseas production subsidiary.

In five cases, all the accounting work was done in the UK and while the mean success rating was higher than where little or no control existed, the success rating is only 1.6. It is possible that the fact that accounting is not done by the subsidiary is symptomatic of a lack of delegation of authority and function to the subsidiary and this may result in some stifling of incentive in the subsidiary. However the increase in the mean success rating, to 1.8, is only slight when the accounts are done by the subsidiary and submitted to the UK firms between once and four times a year.

The highest mean success rating was achieved by the twenty firms whose overseas production subsidiaries submitted accounts every month. The rating for these twenty is 2.6 and while twenty is nearly half of the sample of forty-three, the group contained four of the six totally successful subsidiaries and only one failure.

As noted above, the question asked in the interviews showed that the submission of accounts was the most common form of financial control since only seven firms currently also required budget estimates from their subsidiaries. The mean success rating for these seven firms was 2.9 which suggests that on average budget estimates are associated with the more successful subsidiaries. While there could be a cause and effect situation here (in that the subsidiary was so successful that budget estimates and other management techniques became necessary), it is not necessarily the case and the higher success ratings here, as elsewhere, are merely reflecting the presence of more professional management who expect budget estimates as part of their data for understanding and helping the subsidiary. Among the seven, four used half yearly budget estimates and three used yearly estimates. Since a yearly, or even a half yearly, budget need cover no more than the main headings of revenues and expenditures, it did not appear to be a burden to the subsidiaries — but at the same time it does require the managers of the subsidiaries to think about where they are heading.

> **Scenario 7.1.1**   Success rating: '1'
>
> The experience of the Midlands firm supplying engineered parts to customer specifications, referred to in Scenario 4.1.1, provides a useful example of the use of budget estimates and accounts. In 1973 the firm acquired a loss-making concern in Holland. In order to turn around its new subsidiary to profitability, a comprehensive budget was built up in line with manufacturing capacity. This enabled the firm to assess profit potential. The budget was then implemented as a plan for recovery and progress was monitored through monthly accounts. In preparing the budget estimates, the Dutch management is required to put forward capital expenditure requirements for the forthcoming year. Although funds are allocated in the budget, spending decisions have to be justified on each occasion. In the opinion of the chief executive: 'This contrasts with the experience of large companies, where allocation of funds is a sufficient condition for spending, and where funds are lost if they are not spent in the appropriate time period and without this control we would have been lost'.

Another common element of financial control is through the sanctioning of capital expenditure. Accordingly a question was asked to determine how extensive was this control in the management of overseas production subsidiaries. The analysis is in Table 7.2.

In looking at Table 7.2 it must be borne in mind that the capital expenditure allowed to remain under the overseas production subsidiary's control will vary with its size and with the size of the UK parent. Table 7.2 shows the variation in the maximum amount of capital expenditure which the subsidiary is allowed to authorise and instigate—the range of authorised expenditure varies from zero to unlimited! A

Table 7.2

What is the maximum size of any capital investment project that the local board can ratify at the present time without reference to the UK board?

Response	Number of firms	Mean success rating
No limit	7	1.4
Always consultation	11	1.8
Less than £1000	10	2.1
£1001-£20 000	15	2.5
	43	

further point in understanding the table is that while the lowest positive figure mentioned was 'from £10 to £20', the attempt in constructing the table was to differentiate between those subsidiaries with reasonable discretion and those without.

Seven overseas production subsidiaries were in charge of their own investment policies; that is, no limit was imposed on capital expenditure provided this came from overseas production subsidiary funds. The mean success rating of this group was 1.4. Slightly more successful on average were the eleven subsidiaries which always had to consult with the UK parent. Once these two extremes, unlimited expenditure and always consultation, are left the mean success rating begins to climb. As can be seen from Table 7.2, the mean rating increases as the expenditure limit increases. The implication of Table 7.2 is that total freedom and total control are not on average associated with successful overseas production subsidiaries but when some discretion is granted, the subsidiary appears to respond and the average success increases. In general terms, what appeared from the interviews was that the more successful subsidiaries were those in which the parent and subsidiary had evolved a division of decision making responsibility between general strategy, decided by the parent, albeit in consultation, and technical and operational decisions decided by the managers of the subsidiary. Once again however this is merely professional management at work in reaching agreement where success is the basis for the division of responsibilities.

Scenario 7.1.2 Success rating: '2'

In 1960, a firm engineering quality instruments for the capital goods industry set up a manufacturing unit in Australia. From the start the venture was given an Australian identity and today the subsidiary is virtually autonomous. Providing that new investment projects meet a set rate of return on capital employed, Australian management is free to authorise any capital expenditure.

This autonomous policy for the subsidiary is explained by UK management in terms of the problems of managing at a vast distance and allowing trusted persons in charge of the subsidiary to get on with their job of managing. The firm, however, admits that the capital could have been better spent in the UK.

This section looked first at financial control by means of accounts and budget estimates. As in several sections, it could be said that the analysis has done no more than confirm common business sense. The section showed that there was a relationship between the submission of accounts (ranging from 'never' to monthly) and the mean success rating. The most successful subsidiaries were those submitting monthly accounts. In addition, while only seven firms were currently using budget estimates (yearly or half-yearly frequency) they were, again, the firms with the more successful overseas production subsidiaries. There was no evidence in the interviews that monthly accounts or budget estimates were an excessive burden to the subsidiary and since their use is related to success, they should form part of the management of every overseas production subsidiary. The last part of this section looked at the capital expenditure the overseas production subsidiaries were allowed to make without authorisation. Little discretion and absolute freedom were not on average associated with success but there did appear to be a clear response in success when the subsidiary was allowed a realistic level of freedom on capital expenditure.

7.2 Functional control

This section discusses the location of decision making over the various functions performed by the overseas production subsidiary. Not all overseas production subsidiaries perform a full range of functions—one manager admitted that he allowed overseas management 'not a shred of initiative', as they were required to telex the UK for an answer to the smallest query. This attitude was exceptional of course and the section reports upon the location of decision-making responsibility for (1) setting wages; (2) labour training; (3) purchasing; (4) setting prices; (5) local marketing policy; (6) management recruitment; (7) advertising expenditure decisions; and (8) carrying out research and development.

Table 7.3 shows that, in the majority of cases, overseas production subsidiaries have the decision-making, in all functional areas except research and development. The most common functional area in which the subsidiary has authority is the negotiation of local wage rates; this is true for thirty-eight of the forty-three subsidiaries. Table 7.3 arrays the functional areas according to the number of subsidiaries having the decision–making. The mean success ratings reading across the table do not vary but reading downwards, that is by functional area, the higher success rating is usually associated with the subsidiary having the decision making. However the differences are not large. The exception—both in terms of where the decision-making lies in the majority of cases, and the clear difference in success rating—is in research and development. Only four of the forty-three subsidiaries assist in the overall research and development programme; for the remainder research and development is a parent activity.

Table 7.3 Decision making by functional area

Function	Overseas production subsidiary management	Under control of UK management	Inapplicable
Wages	N* = 38 M* = 2.1	N = 4 M = 2.3	N = 1 M = 1
Labour training	N = 37 M = 2.1	N = 5 M = 2.0	N = 1 M = 1
Purchasing	N = 37 M = 2.1	N = 5 M = 2.0	N = 1 M = 1
Pricing	N = 31 M = 2.2	N = 11 M = 1.9	N = 1 M = 1
Local marketing	N = 30 M = 2.1	N = 11 M = 2.2	N = 2 M = 1.5
Management recruitment	N = 27 M = 2.3	N = 14 M = 1.8	N = 2 M = 0.5
Advertising expenditure	N = 23 M = 2.2	N = 16 M = 2.1	N = 4 M = 1.3
Research & development	N = 4 M = 2.8	N = 38 M = 2.0	N = 1 M = 1

N* = number of firms M* = mean success rating

Note, however, for the four that the mean success rating, at 2.8, is the highest in the table. This reflects the fact that these subsidiaries knowing their own market are able to develop or adapt their own products to those of the market they are serving.

Table 7.4 shows the number of functions controlled by the

subsidiaries and the associated mean success rating. Only one overseas production subsidiary has total independence in the eight functional areas—this is the Australian joint venture in which the UK equity stake has been reduced to a minority twenty-four per cent holding. Sixteen firms maintain UK head office control over research and development but otherwise allow local management to manage the subsidiary. There is not a clear pattern of success and number of functions controlled by the subsidiary. Part of the reason for the lack of pattern is the fact that there are a number of successful

Table 7.4 Number of functions controlled by overseas production subsidiary management

Number of functions under overseas production subsidiary control	Number of firms	Mean success rating
0	4	1.8
2	4	1.3
3	3	2.7
5	6	2.3
6	9	2.2
7	16	2.0
8	1	3.0
	43	

subsidiaries which can be described only as production units in the sense that they are more akin to a factory than to a company. They are able to make decisions only on labour-orientated matters, that is, labour training and the setting of wages. For example, one of these units is the 'offshore plant' in Ireland which conforms to the 'ideal type' of such units, having virtually no functions other than straight production in that the materials, orders and designs are sent to the unit and the manufactured product sent back to the parent firm. While the pattern of success is not clear it is worthwhile pointing out all six of the 'totally successful' subsidiaries have authority in at least five of the eight functions listed.

This section has looked at the functional areas of business to see in which areas the local management has the decision-making authority. The results are not conclusive, but there are

> **Scenario 7.2.1   Success rating: '2'**
>
> After operating an overseas sales subsidiary for a year, a Black Country firm in the silver plating industry opened a finishing and assembly plant in Ireland, from where it hoped to launch a major attack on the large USA market. Functional control is maintained by UK management except in the areas of labour training and the setting of wages, which are under local control. The Irish plant is a branch factory to UK operations and is treated as the poor relation in the group of companies. Investment in Ireland is seen as a mistake, partly because the association the firm hoped to cultivate between its own products and those of an indigenous firm has failed to materialise, partly because of communications and transportation problems, and partly because of the difficulty in maintaining quality control in Ireland.

indications that as more authority is allowed to the local management the success tends to be higher. One area, research and development, stood out as the area in which fewest subsidiaries had any authority but those subsidiaries which did, tended to be the most successful.

7.3 Comparison of control of overseas production subsidiary with UK subsidiaries

In principle the overseas production subsidiary can be controlled in a manner identical to any other subsidiary, such as one in the UK. As a method of comparison, the interviewee was asked to consider the methods of controlling the first overseas production subsidiary and any UK subsidiaries which the firm had. Most answered in terms of more or less strictly controlled or in terms of the degree of autonomy. The balance of replies, as Table 7.5 shows, is slightly tilted towards giving more autonomy to overseas subsidiaries than to UK ones. This is partly felt to be inevitable because of distance and language,

Table 7.5 Comparison of degree of control over overseas production subsidiary with UK subsidiaries

Overseas production subsidiary is:	Number of firms	Mean success rating
Less strictly controlled	14	1.5
Treated exactly as a UK subsidiary	12	2.6
More strictly controlled	6	2.6
No comparison made	11	2.0
	43	

but in some cases represents a conscious policy decision. It was often felt to be preferable to allow the overseas production subsidiary to take the initiative on many issues which would be strictly controlled in a UK subsidiary. Surprisingly, and perhaps mistakenly, the methods of controlling the overseas production subsidiary were frequently described as 'less formal' than those in the UK. Personalised control is easy to implement but is subject to the vagaries of personal relationships and can lead to instability. This perhaps has contributed to the low mean success rating of 1.5 for those less strictly controlled subsidiaries.

For the overseas production subsidiaries which are treated exactly as a UK subsidiary, or are more strictly controlled, the mean success rating is equal at 2.6 and it is substantially higher than for the subsidiaries which are less strictly controlled. For eleven subsidiaries no comparison was made, usually because there were no UK subsidiaries.

In this short section, a simple comparison was made where possible by each interviewee of the control of the overseas production subsidiary and the control of a UK subsidiary. The result of the comparison when the average success ratings are measured is that the overseas subsidiaries which are less strictly controlled than the UK subsidiaries are on average much less successful than those overseas subsidiaries which are treated equal to, or more strictly than, UK subsidiaries. It may simply be a case that distance needs to be counteracted if the subsidiary is to perform well.

7.4 The chief executive

The issue on which the sample is most clearly divided in opinion is that of the nationality of the chief executive of the overseas production subsidiary. Many firms felt very strongly that he must be a local in order to understand local business practices, customs and mores — others felt that unless a Briton was appointed, severe communication and control problems would arise. This section reports upon this dichotomy of opinion.

In the outcome, as Table 7.6 shows, a majority — twenty-two firms, chose a local chief executive, and nineteen chose a Briton. There is a slightly higher mean success rating for the

Table 7.6 Nationality of the chief executive of the overseas production subsidiary

Nationality	Number of firms	Mean success rating
British	19	2.2
Local national	22	2.0
Other	2	1.5
	43	

subsidiaries which had a Briton as the chief executive but the six totally successful firms were equally divided between the two categories.

The arguments, as stated by those interviewed, for putting a Briton in charge of the overseas production subsidiary may be paraphrased as follows. The arguments rest on communication and trust. With local managers it is difficult to know what is going on and they are less likely to take orders from UK head office. Less loyalty can be expected from host country nationals and they are not tuned in to the way the UK firm thinks—differences in the philosophy of management across countries may lead to embarrassment of the parent board and Britons are less likely to take risks on the firm's behalf.

The arguments put forward for employing a host country national as managing director may be summarised in like manner. A national is more understanding of local business practices, customs and mores—he will understand the market, the system of competition and most importantly, the language. He will have local contacts and will be able to deal better with host government officials, suppliers and customers, to whose needs he will be more responsive. Local identification and goodwill is more easily achieved with a national.

Given the importance of language differences, it might be expected that the proportion of host-country local chief executives would be greater in non-English speaking countries. This is not the case—the proportion of British to local chief executives of the overseas production subsidiary is eleven to eight in non-English speaking countries and seven to eight in English speaking countries. (See Table 7.7.)

In connection with the incorporation of a company overseas, it is important to realise that the documents which correspond to the British memorandum and articles of association may need more care in drafting than in the UK.

Table 7.7 Nationality of chief executive by area

Nationality	EEC	Australia and South Africa	Other
British	$N^* = 11$	$N = 7$	$N = 1$
	$M^* = 1.8$	$M = 2.9$	$M = 2.0$
Local national	$N = 8$	$N = 8$	$N = 6$
	$M = 1.9$	$M = 2.1$	$M = 1.5$
Other	$N = 2$		
	$M = 1.5$		

N^* = number of firms; M^* = mean success rating

For example, it may be important to list exclusions either in the equivalent of the memorandum and articles or in the chief executive's contract. A graphic illustration of failure in this respect is the firm which found that the chief executive of its overseas production subsidiary had rented the royal palace guard to provide ceremonial escort at his daughter's wedding! As the interviewee noted: 'The cost was not small and there was nothing we could do about it'.

The topic on which the widest disagreement was expressed in the interviews — the nationality of the chief executive of the subsidiary — has been analysed in this section with respect to the success of the overseas production subsidiary. The sample of subsidiaries was approximately equally split between those with a Briton as chief executive and those with a local national. The mean success rating was slightly higher for those with the Briton as chief executive but the difference is not sufficient that a crucial decision, like the choice of chief executive, should be determined on any grounds other than ability.

7.5 Financial policies

When the overseas production subsidiary becomes profitable, and, whenever the subsidiary buys goods or services from the parent, financial policies have to be determined. In the first case the basic policy decision is whether to reinvest in the subsidiary or to remit to the parent; in the second the decision is the price at which the goods and services change hands. This section looks at these policies for the sample firms.

In respect of the reinvestment or remittance of the subsidiary's profits, most firms interviewed had no set policy on which to base the decision on reinvestment or remittance of profits made by the overseas production subsidiary; instead they reinvested or remitted on an *ad hoc* basis. Only two firms had a definite pattern of profits allocation; both set aside profits on a fifty-fifty basis for reinvestment and remittance. Nine firms had been instructed by the exchange control authorities to remit a fixed proportion of overseas profits (normally two-thirds) and at least one firm felt that this stipulation (which was a condition of exchange control permission for outward investment being granted) was damaging

---

Scenario 7.5.1 Success rating: '2'

The Black Country firm referred to in Scenario 7.2.1 provides a useful illustration of the difficulties in obtaining a fair return to the UK. Materials and components transferred to Ireland are invoiced at cost and no royalties or management fees are charges against the subsidiary. Neither is a block charge made for its share of group overheads, and accounting, marketing and purchasing for the Irish operation is at UK expense. Although this is thought to be unfair, UK managers believe that the morale of the Irish operation would collapse without this UK financial support.

---

the overseas production subsidiary. A few firms generally favoured remittance to the UK for other reasons, including the need to boost UK cash flow — in fact were it not for remittance of profits from its overseas production subsidiary, one firm admitted that it would have faced bankruptcy. Nine firms cited the need to build up the overseas production subsidiary to a viable size as the main reason for their preference for reinvestment. Managers often felt that general business prospects were more promising in overseas markets than in the UK, and in cases where the overseas production subsidiary is situated in a hard currency area, managers preferred to keep their money in currencies stronger than sterling.

In all cases the UK head office provides a range of management services for the overseas production subsidiary, which effectively means that the overseas production subsidiary is subsidised at UK expense. Some respondents said that it was difficult to levy such a charge on the subsidiaries because of fear of damaging morale and performance overseas. The firm highlighted in an earlier section as charging its overseas production subsidiary at rates above normal ex-works prices found this to be the only way of making the overseas production subsidiary add to UK cash flow. Many firms had found a number of ways of achieving the charge, the most common of which are the use of royalty payments, block charges in respect to overall company overheads, and management fees. In fact only seven of the forty-three firms in our sample employ *any* of these charges, although a majority of respondents said that they should have made such charges to their overseas production subsidiary.

As most firms had no set pattern of profit allocation, it was not surprising that vague answers were received to the question 'What criteria do you use in the decision to reinvest or remit profits from . . .?'. Of only eleven firms giving definite replies, nine cited Bank of England conditions (which is an externally-imposed criterion) but also mentioned frequently were currency strength, comparative rates of inflation, and taxation. Those firms with a set policy of remittance or reinvestment repeated their earlier comments, with two firms admitting that they always reinvest so as to avoid paying dividends to UK shareholders.

Firms were then asked whether their remitted profits had to date exceeded the investment outlay overseas. Of the eleven overseas production subsidiaries no longer in existence, six had remitted profits to the UK in excess of the capital outlay; the remainder had made an outright loss (see Section 3.6, Table 3.7). For ongoing subsidiaries the extent to which investment outlays have been recouped varied with the profitability and length of existence of the overseas production subsidiary, in addition to any reinvestment or remittance decisions. Many firms felt that they had not yet had time to recoup past investment, although six said they had already done so and eight felt they were unlikely to do so because of transfer pricing strategy (see below).

To summarise, reinvestment and remittance behaviour cannot, in most cases in the sample, be considered to be a definite strategy. Flexibility appeared to be the rule and perhaps rigid rules are not appropriate where exchange rates, tax and company requirements are constantly changing.

The second financial policy to be covered in this section is transfer pricing which is merely the process of setting prices for intra-company trade in both goods and services. As both buyer and seller are part of the same firm, in theory any price can be set and this price can be used to transfer capital within the firm to change relative profit levels, or to achieve other company goals. In practice, however, there are constraints on transfer prices. External constraints are customs and excise bodies, tax regulations and exchange control supervision. Internal constraints are the difficulties of maintaining cooperation and motivation between parent and subsidiary, lack of information, and the management time required to maintain control.

Transfer pricing is clearly of use when there is a large amount of intra-firm trade. This was not the case in many of our sample. Transfer pricing is thus peripheral to the practices of many firms even though, of course, all parent firms supply management services to subsidiaries, for which a charge could be made legitimately. However, each firm was asked 'How do you set the price at which you invoice the subsidiary for materials and components sent from the UK?'. As Table 7.8 shows only eighteen firms had thought out their strategy on internal pricing between the UK and overseas. Success appeared unrelated to the policy. In a majority of cases the UK parent organisation effectively gave its overseas production subsidiary a hidden subsidy by transferring goods at less than arms length prices—in other words the overseas production subsidiary is treated more favourably than other customers. The discounts given to the overseas production subsidiaries varied in size, with five firms sending goods at cost and nine pricing intra-firm trade at cost plus a percentage of handling. A comment which was made several times was that transfer prices were manipulated as a means of keeping down final goods prices in the overseas market in order to gain a strong competitive foothold.

Table 7.8

How do you set the price at which you invoice the subsidiary for goods received from the UK?

Price at:	Number of firms	Mean success rating
Cost	5	1.8
Cost plus a percentage for handling	9	2.6
Arms length	2	0.5
To achieve a 10% return on value added	1	2.0
Normal ex-works price plus 17½%	1	3.0
No policy decision	25	
	43	

Only two firms manipulated transfer prices to the UK's advantage; one of these adjusted its prices in order to achieve a ten per cent return on value added whilst the other *added* seventeen and a half per cent to normal ex-works prices in order to get capital back to the UK from the overseas production subsidiary. In this particular case the overseas production subsidiary is not allowed by its articles of association to purchase its raw materials from anyone else than its UK parent.

Transfer pricing is a flexible tool which can be used in a variety of ways to transfer funds, shift profits, reduce the overall tax bill, take advantage of changing currency rates, or as a competitive device. For the sample firms which had taken policy decisions on transfer pricing, the most common decision was to set prices so as to give a competitive edge to the final prices charged by the subsidiary. (Because of this element of subsidy to the subsidiary the subsidiary should be assessed at a higher rate of return than previously indicated. Earlier it was said that the return on overseas operations should exceed that of home operations to compensate for the extra risk of operating overseas—to this must now be added a premium to cancel the effects of the 'discount' on goods and services supplied by the UK firm.)

This section has looked at two financial policies for which clear, well-thought out decisions would bring advantages in the operation of an overseas production subsidiary. A policy decision on reinvestment or remittance would give increased certainty in planning the operations of both parent and subsidiary and would clearly indicate goal priorities that each management could work toward. A policy decision on transfer pricing would again set goal priorities to which each management could address itself and would represent a powerful device for achieving stated financial objectives. However in both policies, the majority of firms in the sample had taken no policy decisions. For those firms with stated policies, then in the case of reinvestment or remittance there was no common policy and in the case of transfer pricing favouring prices to the subsidiary to give it a competitive edge in its own final prices was the most common policy. The final verdict must however be that these two financial policies are under-used by smaller firms with overseas production subsidiaries.

7.6 Intra-firm trade

The establishment of an overseas production subsidiary increases the possibilities for the firm to purchase raw materials and intermediate goods in more than one country and to service final markets from more than one location. This section reports upon the extent to which these possibilities have been taken up by the forty-three firms.

Taking purchasing policy first, in order to judge how far the overseas production subsidiaries have been able to meet their input requirements from the host country, firms were asked where they purchased the major bought-in components of production (1) in the initial stages of production and (2) in the current year, or final year in the case of overseas production subsidiaries sold or closed down. Table 7.9 shows the results of this enquiry. Seventeen firms began by importing inputs from

Table 7.9

In the first year of operations in the . . . plant was the bought-in component of production mainly imported or was it mainly purchased in . . .? In the current year has the main source changed?

In first year of operations	In current or final year of operation	Number of firms
Imported from UK	Imported from UK	9
Imported from UK	Purchased in host country	17
Purchased in host country	Purchased in host country	11
Purchased in host country	Imported from UK	1
Imported from a 3rd country	Imported from a 3rd country	4
Not relevant		1
		43

the UK, but by the 'current' or final year had switched to purchasing within the host country. Eleven firms had purchased the bulk of their inputs within the host country from the beginning. Nine firms were continuing to import their major requirements from the UK (usually on favoured terms relating to high quality sub-assemblies or components). One overseas production subsidiary switched against the trend from purchasing locally to importing inputs from the UK because of dissatisfaction with the quality of inputs available. (Another firm was contemplating this action at the time of the interview for similar reasons.)

In general then, many overseas production subsidiaries undergo a reorientation of input purchasing, coming to rely more on local suppliers except for specialised, high quality inputs from the parent firm or trusted suppliers in the UK. This reorientation has the advantages that it reduces transport costs, provides a better integration with the local business community and pleases the host government. The only disadvantage noted in the survey was that of quality control when the switch to local purchasing was made.

Looking now at sales, setting up an overseas production subsidiary provides the firm with opportunities to carry out a 'sourcing policy'. That is, it allows markets to be serviced from more than one location of production. How this is carried out depends on the internal organisation of the firm. Overseas production subsidiaries may be set up (1) to substitute for exports from the UK, (2) to provide a new base for servicing the UK market at cheaper cost (offshore production), (3) to divide third country markets between the parent and the subsidiary or (4) to complement and strengthen parent UK exports by finishing or adaption carried out abroad. The vast majority of the sample fall into the first and fourth categories. As Table 7.10 shows, most firms do not use the overseas production subsidiary to service the UK market. Fifteen firms

Table 7.10

Since the production began in . . . have this company's imports to the UK from . . . increased, remained the same, or declined?

	Number of firms
Imports to UK increased	15
Remained the same	2
Declined	0
No imports to the UK at any time	26
	43

have taken the opportunity at some time to export goods from the overseas production subsidiary to the UK. These are not always finished goods, they may be intermediate goods or components. In the case of two firms, establishment of the overseas production subsidiary has not altered the value of imports made by the parent — although the nature of the imports has altered. One firm imports a sophisticated intermediate good from the host country, whilst the other, instead of importing raw materials, now imports semi-finished goods from the overseas production subsidiary. Twenty-six firms have not, at any time, imported from the host country, although two firms are contemplating such action. As indicated above, only one firm has attempted to divide its product range between the overseas production subsidiary and the parent firm. Such a policy would normally only be carried out when the overseas production subsidiary is well established and has proved its ability in particular product lines in terms of both quality and relative (to the UK parent) cost. One firm hived off an intermediate process (to Ireland) and was re-importing for finishing in the UK. Two other firms use Ireland as an export base (profits from exports are tax free under the Irish industrial incentive schemes).

Scenario 7.6.1   Success rating: '1'

The small firm mentioned in Scenario 5.1.1, operating in one part of the heavy metals industry, has attempted to develop a sourcing policy which allows it to service markets from more than one location of production. When the overseas production unit was established, refurbished UK machine tools were sent out to 'tool up' the operation. The entire UK capacity to 'work' metals to broader specifications was exported, along with some machine tools of narrower technical specification. Market demand for broad specifications in both the UK and Europe is now supplied from the Belgian unit, whereas the more buoyant market demand for 'narrower products' can be met from either the UK or the Belgian plant. In these cases the choice of unit of supply is decided after careful consideration of exchange rates and production schedules.

The effect on UK parent exports, of course, depends on how far the production of the overseas subsidiary is complementary with that of the parent. Where the overseas subsidiary produces goods previously exported from the UK, the export of final goods declines, but this may be compensated for later by increased demand from the overseas unit for intermediate goods. An additional possibility is that the setting up of the overseas production subsidiary may provide a 'piggy back' to exports of other goods in the UK firm's range, produced in the UK, by increasing awareness of the firm's products abroad. Reference to Table 7.11 shows that, in the majority of cases,

Table 7.11

Since production began in . . ., have this company's exports to . . ., increased, remained the same, or declined?

	Number of firms
UK exports to . . . have increased	24
UK exports to . . . have remained the same	8
UK exports to . . . have declined	9
No UK exports at any time to . . .	2
	43

the establishment of an overseas production subsidiary has had a stimulating effect on exports from the parent. In nine cases the overseas production subsidiary has substituted for exports from the UK.

The general conclusion on international intra-firm trade must be that opportunities are often missed. The overseas production subsidiary provides a useful bridgehead for launching suitable products from the parent firm's range—it can in other words also operate as a sales subsidiary. The overseas production subsidiary can also, and should, be used to service third country markets where relative costs justify. Only one firm in the sample had a coherent sourcing policy. Even the firms with smaller overseas production units might benefit from reassessing the network between production sources and final markets, with a view to reducing costs and opening up new markets. The impression gained from the interviews is that this lack of attention is partly due to inability to regard the overseas production subsidiary as an integral part of the firm; and until it is regarded as an integral part, opportunities, and profits, will be sacrificed.

Executive summary

Setting up an overseas production subsidiary is a major step in the growth of the smaller firm but the real challenge comes in controlling the subsidiary. The subsidiary operates in a foreign environment, perhaps a great distance away, yet it must be managed in line with the parent firm's methods, procedures, understanding and aspirations. This chapter has looked at the ways adopted by the forty-three firms in the sample for controlling their overseas production subsidiaries.

In Section 7.1, the emphasis was upon control through the submission of accounts and budget estimates, by the subsidiary to the parent and through the supervision of capital expenditure. There appeared to be a relationship between the submission of accounts and the success of the subsidiary. The subsidiaries which submitted monthly accounts were on average the most successful ones. While nearly all the subsidiaries submitted accounts to the parent only seven submitted budget estimates; these tended to be the more successful subsidiaries. In respect of control over capital expenditure, success was again linked with a realistic measure of control. In fact, little discretion for the subsidiary and absolute freedom for the subsidiary were both associated with low levels of success, while some measure of control was associated with higher levels of success.

In Section 7.2 functional control was examined and generally the conclusions, though not strong, were that the more areas of functional control—local wages, labour training, purchasing, local prices, local marketing, management recruitment, research and development — under the authority of the subsidiary, the more successful the subsidiary. It appeared particularly that where the subsidiary had some authority over research and development, it tended to be successful, presumably because it was able to design its products to local demand.

An overseas production subsidiary can be treated exactly like a UK subsidiary and Section 7.3 analysed whether the two were treated differently. In terms of success, the mean rating was lower for those overseas production subsidiaries less strictly controlled than a UK subsidiary when compared with overseas production subsidiaries treated equally or more strictly than UK subsidiaries.

The choice of the nationality of the chief executive — a contentious point in the interviews — was examined in Section 7.4 and nationality did not appear to be related to the success of the subsidiary to an extent that would encourage any firm to choose other than the best man available.

Financial policies were the concern of Section 7.5 and in respect of the remittance or reinvestment of subsidiary profits and in respect of transfer pricing, the overall conclusion was that the firms in the sample had not used either policy to the extent that they could be used with benefit to the goals of the firm.

The final section, 7.6, looked at the development of trade between the parent and the subsidiary. While the existence of the subsidiary gives the opportunity for flexibility to the *whole* enterprise in purchasing, production and sales, a conclusion similar to that for Section 7.5 must be entered. The sample firms typically had not reached the stage when they regarded the overseas production subsidiary as an integral part of the whole enterprise and consequently were forgoing economies and benefits by not co-ordinating the two units.

To an extent the real challenge in going international is not in conceiving the idea nor putting it into effect but is in successfully and continuously managing the subsidiary in the face of a strange environment and strong competition. In this real challenge, appropriate control procedures by the UK firm over its subsidiary not only allows the UK firm to know the subsidiary and thereby help it but appears on the basis of this survey to be beneficial to the subsidiary itself.

8 Lessons and problems

A structure has been imposed on the firms' responses so that each chapter, from Chapter 4 onwards, represents a succeeding stage in the total process of initiating, setting up and running an overseas production subsidiary. There remains only this chapter which covers the firms' responses on their own view of the total process. Thus this chapter looks at the lessons learned and the problems encountered by the forty-three firms with their first overseas production subsidiaries.

This chapter has some especial significance in that the questions required the managers being interviewed to think of the lessons and the problems themselves without prompts from the interviewer. Thus the managers are reporting the experiences they have selected as useful to be passed on to other managers about to venture abroad. For example, Section 8.1 reports upon the most important lesson learned by the respondents and upon other lessons learned. Section 8.2 looks at subsidiaries set up overseas subsequent to the first production subsidiary with the aim of seeing the importance of the experience with the first subsidiary. Section 8.3 examines the success ratings of the subsidiaries in relationship to the size of the UK firm and its ownership to establish whether either is a necessary prerequisite to success in going international. The final section, Section 8.4, is similar in approach to Section 8.1

but in fact reports upon the most major problems encountered and other less major problems.

8.1 Lessons learned

In response to the question: 'With the benefit of hindsight, what was the most important lesson learned?', two firms said they had learned nothing! They were rated 'average success' and 'not successful' on the scale laid down in Chapter 4. They had thus not experienced total success or outright failure, with the extra learning that success stimulates or failure enforces. However the other forty-one firms did respond positively to this question and the responses are reported in some length here. The length reflects the importance of this section to other firms who wish to utilise the benefits of experience.

The responses are shown in shortened form in Table 8.1 and are grouped for convenience. The group with the most responses is that in which the learning is best described as relevant to the UK firm in general, that is, its head office (Group 1). In this group the most common lesson learned concerns the difficulties of owning and managing at a distance. As one of the five firms said: 'In hindsight we realise now that you don't try and control an overseas production subsidiary by means of one executive director five thousand miles from the action'. And another responded 'The most important lesson we learned was how to manage at long range. We now have three other situations abroad and we learned how to manage these by managing that first overseas production subsidiary'. It seems that here in this section the lessons from Chapter 7 concerned with management and control of the overseas production subsidiaries can only be repeated for emphasis: a formal system of regular reporting is necessary, with personnel making trips in both directions, and beyond that the overseas production subsidiary has to be allowed to run itself as it best can in the local conditions of

Table 8.1

With the benefit of hindsight, what was the most important lesson learned?

Lesson relates to:	Number of firms
(1) UK head office in general ways:	**15**
Difficulties of owning and managing at a distance	5
Importance of adjusting to the foreign culture	4
Just how good foreign companies are	1
Importance of strict financial control	2
Importance of strict technical control	1
Need to plan in more detail	1
Importance of being able to speak the language	1
(2) UK head office in particular ways:	**6**
Difficulties inherent in joint ventures	1
Necessity of having at least 51% of shares	1
Paid too high a price for acquisition	2
It is possible for us to make mistakes	1
Don't believe all you're told	1
(3) Top management of overseas production subsidiary:	**10**
Importance of finding the right man to run the overseas production subsidiary	4
Importance of having a local man to run the overseas production subsidiary	3
Importance of having a UK man to run the overseas production subsidiary	2
Importance of having two men to run the overseas production subsidiary	1
(4) Marketing and the overseas production subsidiary:	**8**
Delayed too long before producing there	2
Went in before market ready	1
Not sensible to manufacture overseas	1
Importance of exploring market first	1
Importance of finding whether customers will pay premium for quality	1
Importance of getting initial scale of production right	1
Importance of having a broader product base	1
(5) Other aspects of the overseas production subsidiary:	**2**
The expense of manufacturing overseas	1
The need to get the location right	1
(6) Nothing	**2**
	43

culture and competition. Day-to-day control, which for domestic operations means that the UK chief executive asks the right questions and, by his presence, is generally aware of problems, cannot work for an overseas production subsidiary.

A smaller number of firms, four, reported that the most important lesson they learned was the importance of adjusting *their* methods and attitudes to those of the culture in which the overseas production subsidiary existed. One firm summed it up by saying:

> 'American is not the same as English, there is a different culture in the USA, they have different priorities there and business methods are different — the overseas production subsidiary was failing until we realised this and gave the subsidiary the autonomy it needed to change its own priorities and methods to fit the US scene.'

Another said:

> 'The way of business is so different (in Italy); standards of business, workmanship and commerce are different. We expected certain standards to be maintained; when we asked they said "Yes, we're doing it", but what they did bore no relation to the standards we'd set down. The crunch came when we visited the plant . . . Also there is a national sport called tax evasion, which involves keeping more than one set of books; the taxman is so used to gross underestimation that if you reveal the real profit he'll take it all in tax — the audit fees for the Italian subsidiary come to more than the audit fees for all our other operations combined.'

One firm summarised its learning by saying that they realised, once they had begun to operate in the home territory of their competitors, just how good their competitors were.

Going International

The respondent summed it up in this way:

> 'The whole company has been professionalised. We have learned the quality of the race in which we were running. The whole presentation of our company was bad in comparison with our German competitors. To be successful in West Germany, you need to present yourselves in an efficient, businesslike manner—this is the reason, I think, why many UK firms look poor at the side of European firms. It extends down even to the good design and quality of the business card you present when calling—we've learned to give attention to detail, to look harder at our products and to ask just what the user wants from them; our customers made constructive comments, we used these comments and made our products more saleable. The West German operation has improved the whole group and the products of the whole group.'

And as another firm noted as a secondary lesson: 'We've learned a lot from them, we've gained expertise and we're now less parochial than our UK competitors; we have different attitudes now, our staff have a broader outlook and are prepared to "go" with the firm'.

The remaining five firms in the group whose learning can be summarised as applying most to the UK head office, summarised the learning as the necessity of having strict financial control (two firms, including one which learned this after some particularly bad debts in Australia in 1974), the importance of having strict technical control (one firm, learned after recurrent complaints from customers in South Africa), the need to plan in more detail (one firm, caused by a specific problem occurring in relation to the racial situation in South Africa), and, fifth, the need to be able to speak the local language (one firm, in relation to bringing Belgians over to the UK plants for training, orientation, etc.).

The second grouping in Table 8.1 relates to lessons learned at the UK head office in particular, rather than general, ways. The group consists of six firms, of which two noted the lessons they learned from being involved in a joint venture, one noting the general problems of joint ventures, and one stating that in future any joint venture must be one in which they have at least fifty-one per cent of the shares. Joint ventures have been discussed in Section 5.1 and perhaps here one firm's learning from its particularly unhappy experience describes the situation:

> 'Joint ventures don't work. In our case the Belgian people were not aggressive enough and we blamed them for the production problems, for they looked after production, and they blamed us for sales problems, which were our primary responsibility. It is bad enough in any firm when the production people blame the sales people and vice versa, but when they are different nationalities as well . . . In France we intend to run our own show; before Belgium we believed smaller firms should go for joint ventures to share the risk, but in Belgium we found we weren't sharing the benefits.'

For two firms in this group, the main lesson learned was that they had paid too high a price for the operations they had bought as their first venture overseas; as this failing seems to apply to all UK firms*, these two are not exceptional. One other firm said its most important lesson was that after years of success in the UK, they found they could make mistakes! The final firm in this group simply noted that they were now more critical and checked facts for themselves having in the course of setting-up the overseas production subsidiary believed too often what they were told.

---

*See G. D. Newbould, *Management and Merger Activity*, Guthstead, 1970, Chapter 2.

The third grouping of lessons learned, shown in Table 8.1 relates to the top management of the overseas production subsidiary. It can be seen that the most common single response in this group is a statement of the importance of finding the right man to run the overseas production subsidiary. The next two entries in the table, after that response, cover a point already discussed (Section 7.4). This is the question of whether a local or a Briton should head the overseas production subsidiary. The table shows that for three firms the most important lesson was that the overseas production subsidiary should be run by a local, while two firms favour a Briton in charge of the overseas production subsidiary. Resolution of the argument was avoided previously and it is intended to do so again; perhaps if these five firms are put with the four who said that it is important to find the *right* man, then nine firms found their main lesson in running an overseas production subsidiary to be the crucial importance of the ability of the chief executive of the overseas production subsidiary. The problem was summarised by one firm: 'It must be the problem that most firms hit; the key decision is the employment of the top man to run it. We made a mistake first and replaced him with a good man. At that distance, he has got to be good and you have to trust him.'

The next grouping in Table 8.1 refers to marketing and the overseas production subsidiary. Sections 6.1 and 6.2 stressed the importance of the product-price-strategy decision in respect of the overseas production subsidiary, and the presence of eight firms citing some feature of marketing as the most important lesson learned adds emphasis to these sections. In three of the eight firms, the lesson was essentially one of timing the investment, which is perhaps one of the more difficult decisions in marketing. One firm, which now has three overseas ventures, noted:

> 'We never do it early enough; we like to be in at the start of market growth, but in fact we're usually a bit behind. In the case of the first venture in par-

Lessons and problems

ticular we should have invested abroad before we did, but the apprehension about setting up abroad intimidated us.'

As a balance, perhaps, the firm which went in too quickly should be quoted:

'We set it up too soon. There was a minimum viable scale of production and there wasn't a large enough market in the area to sustain the venture and its capital equipment. We made losses for four years until the market caught up. With hindsight we should have waited until the market was big enough to produce at the break-even level.'

Of the other five firms in this group citing some aspect of marketing as the main lesson learned, it perhaps ought to be noted that there are three whose first overseas production subsidiary are classified as 'failures', which again emphasises the importance of getting the marketing decisions right.

The final group of firms in Table 8.1 cited lessons learned in connection with some aspect of the overseas production subsidiary other than marketing. One had been surprised at the expense of manufacturing overseas: in particular, while the firm had estimated wage costs accurately, it had grossly underestimated the other labour costs of social security, redundancy and injury insurance. The other firm merely noted that location had turned out to be more important than they had formerly believed and would be giving more attention to this in any future venture overseas.

Table 8.2 shows the responses to the next question in the interview: 'Again with the benefit of hindsight, what was the second most important lesson learned?'. Perhaps the main point to make about Table 8.2 is that it is largely a rerun of Table 8.1; the same sort of lessons learned appear in both tables, but the importance of the lesson differs from one firm to the next. One lesson which can be drawn from Table 8.2,

Table 8.2

Again with the benefit of hindsight, what was the second most important lesson learned?

Lesson relates to:

(1) *UK head office in general ways:*
    Difficulties in owning-managing at a distance
    Importance of adjusting to the foreign culture
    Importance of strict financial control
    Need to plan in more detail
    Importance of being able to speak the language
    Need to give subsidiary more autonomy
    Need to give subsidiary more support
    Need to be aware of currency fluctuations
    European countries still nationalistic and insular
    Need to employ locals to advise on laws, rules, regulations, etc.

(2) *UK head office in particular ways:*
    Difficulties inherent in joint ventures
    Don't believe in all you're told

(3) *Top management of overseas production subsidiary:*
    Importance of finding the right man to run the overseas production subsidiary
    Importance of having a local man to run the overseas production subsidiary
    Importance of having a UK man to run the overseas production subsidiary
    Finding right way of paying top man

(4) *Marketing and the overseas production subsidiary:*
    Importance of getting initial scale of production right
    Importance of finding whether customers will pay premium for quality
    Importance of tariffs as a protection
    Local firms more willing to buy from local manufacturer
    Importance of marketing in general

(5) *Other aspects of the overseas production subsidiary:*
    Need to get the location right
    That the whole cost structure is different
    Start-up costs are always higher than expected
    More training necessary

   Note: Column sum would not equal forty-three, as some firms gave more than one secondary problem, some firms none.

rather than Table 8.1, is the need to be aware of the host country environment, culture, business practices and legislation. Knowledge of these can be acquired through the incremental learning process as experience of the country increases through exporting, having an agent, and operating a sales subsidiary. Alternatively, short-cut methods involve information gathering and evaluation. The fact that these host country factors figure so prominently in the table indicates once again that some firms were inadequately prepared for their first overseas production subsidiary.

This section has looked at lessons learned by the respondents in the survey. Tables 8.1 and 8.2 effectively summarise these lessons and they are the type of table, used in some other sections also, which serve best as a checklist for other firms about to venture overseas. The tables summarise actual experiences and one part of successful management is learning from the experiences of others.

8.2 Subsequent ventures overseas

The number and type of ventures overseas subsequent to the first overseas production subsidiary were included in Chapter 3 in the measurement of success of that first subsidiary. The rationale was that one parameter of success of the first subsidiary was the experience and confidence it gave to the UK firm to go overseas again. The aim of this section is to comment upon the subsequent ventures overseas as additional information to the lessons learned in the previous section.

Of the forty-three firms in the sample, twenty-four gained sufficient confidence from their first overseas production subsidiary to set up another thirty-three overseas production subsidiaries and six overseas sales subsidiaries in addition. The details are shown in Table 8.3. One firm has set up three overseas production units subsequent to its first venture in West Germany which is classified as a total success (on the

Table 8.3 Later overseas ventures

After the first overseas production unit, the firm has set up:	Number of firms	
3 overseas production subsidiaries	1	4.0
2 overseas production subsidiaries	9	1.8
1 overseas production subsidiary and 2 overseas sales subsidiaries	1	3.0
1 overseas production subsidiary and 1 overseas sales subsidiary	2	2.0
1 overseas production subsidiary	9	2.1
1 overseas sales subsidiary	2	2.5
	24	2.1

overall success index developed in Chapter 4). Nine firms have set up two other overseas production subsidiaries and nine have established one other overseas production unit. The mean success ratings for the first ventures of these two groups are 1.8 and 2.1 respectively. This suggests that the outcome of the first venture is less important than the experience gained in the process of 'going international'. The overall lack of pattern in the table strengthens this view and in fact, the twenty-four firms which made second and third ventures abroad experienced the whole spectrum of success in their first venture. Included in the twenty-four are three of the 'totally successful' firms and two firms whose first ventures were rated as 'failures' but which can only be described as 'disasters'. A comparison of the mean success ratings of the first ventures of the twenty-four firms setting up subsequent operations abroad with that of the sample as a whole or the nineteen firms which did not again venture overseas yeields similar reinforcement and verification of this hypothesis. The mean success ratings of the three groups are identical — 2.1 — which indicates that firms making later overseas investments had not on average experienced greater success in their first venture. The evidence therefore points to firms undertaking further ventures because they have acquired more of that elusive but important quality — confidence.

The thirty-three subsequent overseas production subsidiaries and the six subsequent overseas sales subsidiaries show a wider spread of country and area than do first ventures. This may be expected because the first experience acquired in operating in an alien environment enables the firm to approach other more 'risky' ventures with greater commitment. In Table 8.4 it is shown that two overseas production subsidiaries have been established in the Third World, India and Nigeria — the first such ventures to occur in the sample firms.

Table 8.4 Later overseas ventures by area

Overseas sales	Overseas production subsidiaries	Overseas sales subsidiaries
Developed Commonwealth		
South Africa	5	1
Canada	2	2
Australia	4	
New Zealand	2	
	13	3
EEC		
France	3	1
Holland	4	
Ireland	2	
Belgium	1	
	10	1
Rest of Commonwealth		
Malta	1	
India	1	
Nigeria	1	
	3	—
Other		
USA	3	
Mexico	1	1
Spain	1	
Portugal	1	
Norway	1	
Bahamas		1
	7	2
Total ventures	33	6

Both are Commonwealth countries but are still likely to pose problems because of lack of support facilities in the economy. There also appears in the table to be a readiness to attempt to break into the massive USA market—three overseas production subsidiaries and one overseas sales subsidiary were located there. In addition investments in Canada were a springboard to launching an attack on the USA market. Other markets also were new hosts for overseas production subsidiaries—notably, Mexico, Spain and Portugal. Several firms were considering making further investments and among the overseas production subsidiaries about to be launched at the time of the interviews were a joint venture in Japan and two ventures in New Zealand.

While there does appear to be this willingness among the sample firms to be more venturesome, it is still a fact that eleven of the twenty-four firms invested subsequently in the same cultural or economic 'bloc' as the first time. In a sense this is a highly rational strategy since the lessons learned the first time around will be directly applicable to the subsequent investments. The details are given in Table 8.5. Four firms pursued an investment policy centered upon the countries comprising the White Cominions whilst seven firms confined their operations to the EEC. These groups can be judged to have made 'reasonable' investment decisions by applying their

Table 8.5 Comparison of location of first and subsequent ventures

Location of first overseas production subsidiary	Mean success rating of first venture	Location of later venture	Number of firms
White Dominions	3.0	EEC	2
White Dominions	2.8	White Dominions	4
White Dominions	1.5	Other	2
EEC	1.0	White Dominions	2
EEC	2.1	EEC	7
EEC	2.0	Other	4
Other	2.0	EEC	2
Other	2.0	White Dominions	1
			24

experience of the economic or cultural block to its other constituents. Unlike the EEC which is an economic bloc with wide cultural differences between member nation-states, the White Dominions have strong cultural and kinship ties which undoubtedly generate trading relationships. However, it is only in terms of Commonwealth Preference that the White Dominions, excluding South Africa, can be linked economically. Thirteen firms set up later ventures outside the economic or cultural block of the first overseas production subsidiary. Willingness to invest in different competitive and market environments can be used as an indication of the degree of confidence gained by the firm in operating in alien conditions and forms one stage in the development of a firm's international strategy.

While there is not sufficient detail given in Table 8.5 to detect the fact, it is the case that only two firms have concentrated their overseas investment policy towards one country. Both have taken over further enterprises in the host countries — Holland and South Africa — and widened the spread of their activities. The firm whose overseas investment strategy is to build up operations in Holland prefers Holland to other EEC countries because of its 'superior managerial competence and national characteristics', although the product is marketed throughout Europe. The second investment enabled the firm to integrate the printing of fabric into its production process of garment manufacture and reduce the value of bought-in fabric. The South African case is very different — further investments reflect the difficulties of repatriating capital from South Africa and of applying South African experience to other countries. Consequent to these problems, the firm has moved into new market segments in South Africa.

Of the remaining firms most established operations in second and third countries similar to the first overseas production subsidiary. These firms typically extend their activities horizontally, producing the same or similar products in different market environments using the same technology.

However a new technology base was acquired by one firm making its new overseas investment in Holland. The takeover enabled the firm to penetrate a parallel and complementary market which did not compete with its mainstream products manufactured in the UK. Another firm, referred to elsewhere in the text, set up later operations in the USA and Mexico, where its existing technology could be applied to new market segments. In the USA the technology is adapted towards the separation and clarification of mineral oils, whereas in Mexico activity is concentrated in the sugar industry. The international strategy of this firm is based on identifying profitable opportunities for applying its technology in new market segments.

It could be expected that later overseas ventures will be more successful than first ventures because of the experience acquired and the lessons learned and problems encountered in the first venture. However, lessons and problems are also learned and encountered in second and third ventures through experience of new conditions and environments.

Three firms, who had (very different) experiences in South Africa where their first overseas production units were located, later began operations in Australia. None of the three Australian ventures was successful and all were closed. One of the firms, whose first investment was rated 'not successful' on the composite success rating scale developed in Chapter 4, sold off its South African operations to a UK competitor when the subsidiary turned in heavy losses. The Australian investment of this firm is seen by the chief executive of the parent company as a mistake:

> 'We didn't do enough market research and we completely ignored any assessment of the competitive structure of the industry which is controlled by three firms. Our entry to Australia provoked a price war with which our new venture was unable to compete. We pulled out.'

A third overseas production subsidiary was set up in New Zealand as a joint venture with a local firm. The UK parent company later sold its share to the local partner because of difficulties of knowing what was happening in New Zealand. With its international strategy in ruins, this firm retrenched into the UK market for a time before venturing back to Australia with an overseas sales subsidiary. Another firm, 'totally successful' in South Africa, also attributes its Australian failure to inadequate acknowledgement of the competitive structure of the industry. The firm was unable to achieve sufficient market penetration to ensure a break-even volume of production in the local plant which was consequently closed. On the basis of these firms' experiences it is clear that the rules of competition still apply. Confidence and experience derived from the first overseas investment do not excuse a sloppy approach to subsequent investments, nor do they ensure success of those later ventures.

Perhaps the most significant comment concerning later ventures is the development by some firms of a definite 'international strategy'. Amongst the forty-three sample members, several are emerging as international firms in the sense that their strategies are related to penetrating as many markets as possible, by establishing production and sales facilities abroad, as well as by exports. It would appear that five firms now have this 'international outlook' and others are feeling their way towards taking an international rather than a UK view on specific issues. One firm, whose first investment was designed to avoid the imposition of a tariff by Australia, was concerned to attack directly the massive USA market and saw an overseas production subsidiary as the best way of achieving this. This was the first stage in a policy of identifying markets worldwide and then investing — a 'search and attack' policy which enables the firm to maintain control over its advanced technology. The later investment in Mexico was triggered by a local content policy by the Government, which is the main customer and now a joint venture partner, and ensures that new orders are put in the way of the overseas production subsidiary. Similarly a firm whose first investment was triggered by the search for raw material inputs also identified the USA market from an overseas production subsidiary in Canada. In addition this firm was establishing a large scale plant in Belgium to begin its assault on the EEC market. Another firm chose to diversify worldwide, choosing the USA as a major target. After investments in West Germany and France (the latter to cope with local differences and xenophobia) overseas production subsidiaries were established in the USA and Canada. Similarly a fourth firm set up its first overseas production subsidiary in South Africa manufacturing its mainstream UK products. However, with its acquisition of a Dutch firm, its international strategy changed from 'finding new markets for existing products' to 'finding new markets for existing products *and* finding new products for existing markets'. The 'new products' are complementary but are not competitive with mainstream UK activities. The fifth firm's 'international strategy' involved the search for a site for an 'offshore plant', that is a production facility sited on low cost labour designed specifically to export back to the UK. The chosen site was Malta.

It has been shown in this section that the success of the first overseas production subsidiary is not related to the willingness of the firm to make subsequent ventures overseas. Thus it appears that confidence is perhaps the main experience gained from the first overseas production subsidiary. Of the forty-three sample firms, twenty-four made subsequent overseas investments to the extent of thirty-three production subsidiaries and six sales subsidiaries; while some mistakes were made among these subsequent ventures, the encouraging sign for other smaller firms is the way that at least five of the smaller firms in the sample have developed already into international firms and others too, in spite of their size, are proving their ability to create an international growth strategy.

8.3 Size and ownership of firm

Throughout, the concern is with the smaller firms and since the conclusion to the previous section commented directly upon size, it is perhaps an appropriate point to look at the impact of size upon success. In addition the type of ownership of the firms will also be analysed in respect of success.

In Chapter 2, which described the sample of forty-three firms interviewed in this survey, size was measured by sales and by numbers employed. Some comment was made at that stage to the effect that some firms currently contemplating 'going international' might be encouraged by the *range* of the size of firms which have already taken the plunge. There were, for example out of the forty-three firms, ten firms with UK sales of less than £2 million, six firms with less than one hundred employees, and four firms with UK sales less than £2 million and less than one hundred employees. In this section, the size of the UK firm will be related to the sucess of the overseas production subsidiary. The data are in Table 8.6. Looking

Table 8.6 Size of firm

Sales £m.	\ 1-100	Numbers 101-400	employed 401-900	\ 901-1500	\ 1501+	All
Less than 2.0	N* = 4 M* = 2.0	N = 6 M = 1.8				N = 10 M = 1.9
2.1-4.0	N = 1 M = 1	N = 5 M = 2.0	N = 6 M = 2.0			N = 12 M = 1.9
4.1-6.0		N = 1 M = 4	N = 3 M = 1.7	N = 1 M = 3		N = 5 M = 2.4
6.1-8.0		N = 1 M = 3	N = 4 M = 2.3			N = 5 M = 2.4
8.1-10.0	N = 1 M = 0		N = 2 M = 0.5	N = 4 M = 3.3	N = 4 M = 2.3	N = 11 M = 2.1
All	N = 6 M = 1.5	N = 13 M = 2.2	N = 15 M = 1.8	N = 5 M = 3.2	N = 4 M = 2.3	

N* = number of firms   M* = mean success rating

first at the rows which classify by sales, it can be seen that there is no marked tendency for the mean success rating to increase as the sales size of the firm grows (namely, mean success ratings of 1.9, 1.9, 2.4, 2.4, 2.1 in order of increased sales category). Looking now at the columns which shows size by reference to numbers of persons employed, there is equally little impression of a pattern: the mean success ratings are 1.5, 2.2, 1.8, 3.2, 2.3. Finally, looking at the boxes formed by the double size classification, the top left-lower right diagonal (that is, both measures of size increasing) does not show any strong pattern either: 2.0, 2.0, 1.7, 2.3.

Another sample characteristic covered in Chapter 2 was the ownership of the firm. For the three categories of ownership (private limited company, public limited company and quoted public limited company) that existed at the time the overseas production subsidiary was set up, the success ratings of the overseas production subsidiaries are shown in Table 8.7.

Table 8.7 Ownership of firm

	Number of firms	Mean success rating
Private limited	19	2.2
Public limited	9	2.0
Quoted public limited	15	2.0
	43	

There is a range of success for each type of ownership and the table shows the mean for each type bears no relationship between ownership and the success of the overseas production subsidiary.

The conclusion must be that there is no clear relationship between size of (UK) firm and the success of the overseas production subsidiary, nor between the ownership of the firm (even a private company *vis-à-vis* a quoted company). Consequently neither the size of firm nor the ownership status of the firm should be a deterrent to going international.

8.4 Problems encountered

Problems are the substance of management — they make the job interesting and challenging, but equally a part of professional management is action to prevent problems arising. It is with this latter action that this section is concerned, for by reporting the problems encountered by the forty-three firms in setting up their first overseas production subsidiaries, other managers should be able to plan more effectively to avoid similar problems.

One reason why first overseas production subsidiaries were chosen is that more mistakes are likely to be made and more problems encountered in first rather than subsequent overseas production ventures by any one firm. So again some surprise must be expressed when six firms said they had no problems in response to the question: 'What was the most major problem that you encountered in setting up and operating production facilities in . . .?'. However, in view of the comments made in previous sections where 'nil' responses have been reported, it is no longer a surprise to record that the mean success rating for the firms encountering no problems is low; in fact there is one '4' (totally successful) holding up the average considerably since the next highest rating is a '2' (average success), the remaining firms scoring less. In the case of the '4' firm, it did appear an accurate description that there had in fact been no problems, for it did appear to be a smoothly set-up and a smoothly running operation, but for the remaining firms recording success ratings of '2' or less, the absence of problems perhaps reflects that the survey is recording perceptions rather than hard events, and what is a problem to one manager may not appear to be worth reporting to us by another manager —

or possibly he had not observed the presence of the problem!

Other than these six, the remainder of the forty-three firms did report their most significant problem; these are summarised in Table 8.8.

The table shows that the most common problem relates to the employment of the workforce. Eleven firms reported some aspect of labour employment as their most major problem, and of these, six had their major problem in respect of training. Most commonly this was a straightforward problem that the local workers had no heritage of skill in the particular tasks required, nor had they been trained by the government

Table 8.8

What was the most major problem that you encountered in setting up production facilities in . . .?

Problem	Number of firms
Labour:	11
Training of local workers	6
Shortage of workers for training	4
Disputes	1
Managerial:	5
Finding right top man	3
Relationships with partners	2
Financial:	5
Taxation, funds transfers, etc.	3
Valuation of stock taken over	1
Cost of factory	1
Production:	7
Quality control in own works	3
Quality control in subcontracting	1
Supplies of raw materials etc. from UK	3
Marketing:	3
Trying to generate enough sales	1
Generating initial sales	2
UK head office:	6
Drain on cash flow	1
Drain on UK people	1
Controlling subsidiary	2
Attitude of head office to subsidiary	2
None:	6
	43

Lessons and problems

for the new tasks, and the firm had to spend time and money doing the training; in all cases the problem became the 'most major' because the time and money expended were greater than anticipated. In one case (in Eire) the problem was compounded by recurrent strikes, and in another case the problem was rather more specialised. The firm had set up its overseas production subsidiary in France and reported that in the locality good trained labour was available and within the factory the workforce was more flexibile than in the UK and the tradesmen worked to a better standard than their UK counterparts, but the problem arose when the product was sent for installation in customers' premises. The only men prepared to do this work were not the best (in fact they were 'guestworkers'—local labour refused to work away from home), and once away from the factory and supervision they worked at their own pace. Further, the high rate of turnover of these men meant the firm was involved in continuous training.

Four firms under the heading of 'labour' in Table 8.8 reported a shortage of workers as their most major problem. One firm had been established in Luxembourg since 1958, and with the growth of the overseas production subsidiary and the industrial growth of Luxembourg the pool of local labour had effectively dried up, and the firm reported that labour of any type—skilled or unskilled—was difficult to get. They in fact were now using immigrant workers and no fewer than five languages were spoken on the shopfloor. Another firm, which set up its subsidiary in Australia in 1962, had the same experience of change over time in the local labour market and now only had recent immigrant labour available to it, and even this was scarce.

For five firms the most significant problem was essentially managerial and, as shown in Table 8.8, for three of these firms the problem was simply one of finding the right man to run the overseas production subsidiary. It is primarily discussions with these firms that have led to the conclusion that the concern over whether a local or a Briton should be in charge ought to be subsumed into a problem of simply finding a good top man regardless of his nationality. The remaining two firms of these five reported relationships with partners as their most major problem; these firms' problems have been covered effectively in Section 5.1 dealing with joint ventures.

Financial problems were the major ones for five firms; three reported their most major problem as the laws, rules and regulations concerning such matters as tax in the foreign country, particularly in relation to its treatment by the UK tax authorities and transfer of funds between the overseas production subsidiary and the UK. However, in one case it must be reported that the problems were personal rather than associated with the firm, in that the shareholder/manager in the UK had changed his residence status as defined by UK tax and UK exchange control regulations.

Under the heading of production problems, named by seven firms, quality control was the most important production problem for four firms. In three cases, one in West Germany, one in Italy and one in Australia, the problem was quality control in their own factory; but for the other firm in South Africa, the problem was one of obtaining a consistent supply of components from subcontractors to the required standards. For the remaining three firms in this fourth entry in Table 8.8, the main production problem was in ensuring an orderly and regular supply of raw materials or other products from the UK to the overseas production subsidiary.

Three firms had their most major problem in the area of marketing: for one it was simply a problem of generating enough sales to occupy the plant they had put down, and in fact the firm has given up the struggle and pulled out. In respect of the other two firms, one had difficulties in the USA until it learned to be more aggressive in its selling activities, and the other timed its entry into Belgium rather badly with the result that purchasing firms tended to buy from their existing suppliers rather than the newcomers.

The final group of six firms in Table 8.8 had major problems which can be effectively summarised as relating to the UK head office. Two firms were involved in considerable

Lessons and problems

underestimation. In one case the underestimation was of the cash needed by the overseas production subsidiary, and, in the other, of the frequency of visits and the number of people involved in flying over to look after the overseas production subsidiary. For two firms the most significant problem was simply one of how to control the subsidiary and since one subsidiary was in France and one in Germany, it was not simply distance that was causing the problem but rather the wishes of the local management to 'do their own thing'. For the remaining two firms in this group it was a question of changing the attitude of the people in the UK who looked upon and treated the overseas production subsidiary as a Cinderella (that is, before the coach arrived).

Table 8.8 is supplemented by Table 8.9 which shows the second most major problem encountered by the firms. Many of the problems are reoccurrences of those in Table 8.8, indicating their frequency and the fact that the size of the problem differs from firm to firm.

The tables in this section are useful as a warning device and their value is increased by the fact that many of the problems encountered by the firms were *avoidable*. Thus, for example: the availability and skill of workers in a locality can be checked by visiting the local employment exchange and by talking to other firms in the area; finding the right chief executive ought to be done before the plant is set up; financial regulations are by and large written down and experts can be consulted; production problems will not be unique to your venture, other firms in that locality (or that country) will have the same problems and asking around will clarify the extent of the problem; marketing problems — certainly of the type reported here — simply should not arise if the firm follows a slow route or follows up its export strategy and customers (Section 4.1); and the head office problems reported here should not be unexpected. These comments will not apply to every firm in the sample, and of course problems will always occur no matter how great the preparation to avoid them, but there are clear indications in Tables 8.8 and 8.9 of simply

Table 8.9

What was the second most major problem that you encountered in setting up and operating production facilities in . . .?

Problem

Labour:
   Training of local workers
   Shortage of workers for training
   Disputes
Managerial:
   Finding right top man
   Relationship with partners
   Lax supervision of workers by foreman etc.
Financial:
   Taxation, funds transfers etc.
   Lower margins
Production:
   Quality control in own works
   Supplies of raw materials etc. from UK
   Finding suitable factory
   Quality control in subcontracting
Marketing:
   Adjusting sales techniques
UK head office:
   Drain on cash flow
   Drain on UK people
   Controlling subsidiary
   Language difference

Note Column sum would not equal forty-three, as some firms gave more than one secondary problem, some firms none.

inadequate preparation, and the avoidance of this mistake will be helped by a study of the two tables.

Executive summary

This is the last chapter in a series of five dealing with the setting-up and the running of an overseas production subsidiary. It dealt with the learning inherent in an overseas production subsidiary.

In Section 8.1, the responses to questions on what the UK firm had learned from its overseas production subsidiary were reported. Since the questions were open-ended it is likely that the learning reported in Tables 8.1 and 8.2 will be found to occur in other firms which are about to go international; accordingly study of the tables will allow the learning process to be shortened.

In Section 8.2 subsequent overseas ventures were analysed and it appeared that confidence was perhaps the main thing to emanate from the first overseas production subsidiary since subsequent ventures were undertaken irrespective of the success of the first. Although a detailed analysis of the success of later ventures is beyond the scope of this book, and while there were some mistakes, it was apparent that there are fewer failures or closures amongst later investments. What must be particularly encouraging to managers of other smaller firms is the number of firms in the sample which had clearly developed an international strategy and in spite of their size could be fairly described as international firms.

Section 8.3 picked up the question of size and showed that neither it, nor the ownership characteristics of the firm, were related to success. Thus a small private limited firm is not precluded, on the basis of this sample, from successfully going international.

The final section reported the problems encountered by the forty-three firms with their first overseas production subsidiary. The main point to emerge from Tables 8.8. and 8.9 was that many of the problems were avoidable ones and thus they can form a pre-investment checklist for other firms about to commit money overseas.

In five chapters, many aspects of setting-up and running an overseas production subsidiary have been related to the success of the subsidiary. No amount of reading of the five chapters will guarantee success for a firm about to venture overseas, but it is likely that intelligent application of the findings of this survey will tilt the scales toward greater success than would have been achieved otherwise. One other thing is clear — smaller firms have great opportunities overseas.

9 Overseas sales subsidiaries

As noted in Chapter 2, the survey was set up to deal with overseas production subsidiaries. However, a number of firms contacted in the enquiry stages expressed a willingness to participate even though they had set up an overseas sales subsidiary only. Consequently, in order not to let potential data slip by, there was a follow up on these firms. Thus, this chapter examines the experiences of smaller firms which have recently established marketing and distribution subsidiaries abroad for the first time. The purposes of the chapter are to determine the extent to which an overseas sales subsidiary is a potential springboard to overseas production, and to determine the extent to which a local presence and sales facility generates demand for the firm's products. Lessons learned and problems encountered are discussed in order to assist those managers currently contemplating setting up an overseas sales subsidiary for the first time.

The methodology of this chapter is the same as in the case of setting up an overseas production subsidiary. However the depth of analysis is not as great. One reason is that the sample covers only nine firms and hence the influence of chance is greater than with forty-three firms and conclusions must be less definite. Another reason is that setting up an overseas sales subsidiary is a less complicated operation and an overseas sales subsidiary does not represent as great a resource commitment as does an overseas production unit. Indeed, the requirements of a sales subsidiary are very much less in terms of capital, labour and technology. The initial investment sum is by comparison with an overseas production subsidiary very small—usually in terms of only a few hundred pounds. In essence all that is required is a sales office and distribution facilities; in a small market a sales representative could run such an operation from his own home using his own vehicle for deliveries. Given these relatively small start-up costs, a firm is not locked-in to its investment as in the case of a more expensive operation. Write-off would not unduly affect the consolidated balance sheet. Nevertheless no manager likes loss-making operations. A venture should be successful and it is the manager's job to ensure success. The experiences of others are useful to those with no previous international experience of their own in providing a guide to the pitfalls and dangers of setting up abroad. Past experiences are also useful in discerning the important components of 'success'.

As in the case of setting up an overseas production unit, the most important question for the manager is: 'Were the overseas sales subsidiaries successful?'. Following the pattern established in Chapter 4, a range of indicators are given by which it is possible to evaluate comparative performance and judge decisions against an objective yardstick of overall success.

9.1 Success of exports

Growth of export orders is undoubtedly an essential component of overall success and the spectrum of success in growth of export sales due to the overseas sales subsidiaries was wide. For example, two managers were 'astonished' at the way in which the demand for their products increased as a result of their establishing a local facility in the overseas market, and of course there were managers who were disappointed by the lack of success of their subsidiaries in promoting sales. There were however no 'disasters' or 'jokes' as were found in the overseas production subsidiary sample.

In general terms, to justify its existence, an overseas sales subsidiary must generate a more rapid growth of sales in its host country than direct selling or agency representation has elsewhere. Replies to the question: 'Have exports of that main product increased faster to that country than to others where you do not have a sales subsidiary?' are given in Table 9.1. It

Table 9.1 The rate of growth of export sales in the host country of the overseas sales subsidiary

Host country showing faster growth of sales than other overseas markets	5
Host country showing same growth of sales as other overseas markets	2
Host country showing slower growth of sales than other overseas markets	2
	9

shows that the experiences of more than half the sample group are in line with the assumption that an overseas sales subsidiary provides exports sales leverage and stimulus.

Three of the sample group of firms had no previous exporting experience when they decided to set up abroad and therefore were unable to compare growth in the host country market with that in any other overseas market. Although breaking into a new market is never easy it could be argued that overseas growth should at least equal that achieved in the UK. Otherwise the firm would have been 'better off' by expanding in its UK investments which by the nature of proximity and experience are less risky than foreign investments. The three non-exporters are equally spread amongst the three categories in Table 9.1. Second, it may be expected that a local facility would generate goodwill and demand for the firm's products because of customer preference for dealing with locally established firms. Accordingly, an overseas sales subsidiary will generate more export orders, 'other things being equal', because of the firm's involvement with the host country environment. This consideration is double-edged. First, and intuitively, managers were asked whether in their opinion sales have increased faster in the host country than they would have done in the absence of the investment. As Table 9.2 shows only one firm replied

Table 9.2

Do you think exports to the host country have increased faster than they would have done in the absence of the investment?

Yes	8
No	1
	9

negatively, which suggests confirmation, albeit subjective, of the belief that a local presence generates orders. The second and more objective consideration arising from the 'presence effect' is the firm's enhanced ability to introduce and market other products in the host country. These may or may not be mainstream UK products, as the overseas sales subsidiary can act on behalf of other manufacturers. Some evidence is given in Table 9.3, for although sales promotion activities were

Table 9.3 Evidence of change in demand for other products as a result of local presence ('piggy-back effect')

Firms who found increased demand	4
Firms who did not find increased demand	2
Not known	3
	9

naturally concentrated towards particular products, the table suggests that almost half the sample group of firms felt the presence of a 'piggy-back' effect.

The criterion, growth in export orders, which contributes to the overall success index has three components. Although the sample size is small it is indicative that a positive effect on growth in export orders was found by at least half of the firms setting up their first overseas sales subsidiary.

9.2 Success: expectations and objectives

A second important indicator of success is the firm's own evaluation of its subsidiary's performance in terms of meeting expectations and objectives. Expectations are a subjective indicator because of their broad and often vague constituents and they are also affected by the relative optimism or pessimism of the manager. Depsite these drawbacks there is value in the question: 'Has the actual outcome of that first venture exceeded, met or failed to meet the expectations you held for it?'. Replies are tabulated in Table 9.4. It shows a

Table 9.4 Expectations and outcome

Outcome exceeded expectations	2
Outcome met expectations	5
Outcome failed to meet expectations	2
	9

balanced response but in over three-quarters of cases the actual outcome of the venture had met or exceeded expectations.

In terms of performance objectives, all nine firms said that their main objective in setting up the overseas sales subsidiary was to increase export sales and market share in the host country. Firms were then asked to relate achieved performance to objectives. Only two firms had translated broad objectives into laying down sales targets and planned market penetration. Thus a point can be made, as with the overseas production subsidiaries, that objectives or targets were most commonly not defined except in qualitative terms. For the management of the overseas subsidiary, this makes their task either easier or more hard, depending upon their calibre as managers. Without specific objectives and targets it is difficult to do well and difficult to do badly either, and this may appeal to a particular kind of manager. Put at its crudest: sloppy firms attract sloppy managers. With specific and realistic objectives and targets, a good manager will respond and expect to be rewarded, or chided, for his actual performance. Given that seven of the nine firms in the sample did not define objectives or targets, the question becomes subjective and Table 9.5 shows the responses. It shows only one firm felt that

Table 9.5

How did the subsidiary's performance compare with your objectives?

Performance exceeded objectives	1
Performance met objectives	4
Performance met objectives later than anticipated	2
Performance below objectives	2
	9

results were better than expected, whilst three firms said that performance had met objectives and in fact said performance 'compared well' with their objectives, and one 'modest' firm adding that 'according to our competitors' count, we have ninety per cent of the local market for our product'. Others found markets slow to develop and performance objectives were realised much later than originally envisaged. One sales subsidiary however, had failed to meet its original targets, in spite of its fourteen years existence, and the other firm in this category is expected to move into the black in the current year.

In terms of expectations and objectives as criteria of success, the responses are more subjective than might be the case with other samples; nevertheless, the perceptions of success are a valid part of the overall measure of success, and are weighed accordingly in Section 9.4.

9.3 Success: expansion

There are various ways in which expansion of overseas

facilities can indicate the success of the first overseas sales subsidiary. One is actual or planned expansion of the physical facilities of that first overseas sales subsidiary. Another is to use the knowledge, experience and confidence gained from a successful overseas sales subsidiary to make more moves overseas, perhaps by opening sales subsidiaries in other countries.

A firm's success with its investment can be seen from its subsequent willingness to expand the facilities there. Long established overseas sales subsidiaries may have expanded already and more recent investments may only just have achieved a build up to full capacity utilisation in terms of warehousing and distribution facilities but as the age of investments in the sample ranges up to twenty-five years, the indicator of expansion can include both past expansions and future intentions to expand (to allow for the variability of time in the same way as it was allowed for in the case of overseas production subsidiaries). In fact, only one firm did not fulfill this double criterion, suggesting that for the most part firms have had success with their first overseas sales subsidiaries.

The second form of expansion is linked with the strategy of foreign investment itself, as firms who are operating successfully abroad will tend to set up local operations in other countries. As can be seen from Table 9.6, five firms have set

Table 9.6 Later overseas ventures

4 overseas sales subsidiaries	1
2 overseas sales subsidiaries	2
1 overseas sales subsidiary	2
Minority investments in 16 countries	1
No further overseas investments	3
	9

up similar sales and marketing organisations in other countries. One firm has set up four later ventures on its own account, which indicates a substantial degree of involvement and commitment to export sales. Another firm has bought minority equity holdings in distribution facilities in sixteen other countries, but does not have sufficient confidence in its first overseas sales subsidiary to repeat the operation in other overseas markets. Three firms have not undertaken any further foreign investments.

An overseas sales subsidiary can be the platform for the launch of a successful overseas production subsidiary, as shown in Section 4.1. Of the nine firms in this sample, one firm is currently in the process of launching an overseas production subsidiary, introducing initially the final stages of assembly and packaging of completely knocked-down parts exported from the UK. Later it intends to integrate production backwards into local component manufacture. Three others have tentative plans to launch an overseas production unit when annual sales justify such a move. The remaining firms would not consider establishing a production unit abroad for a variety of economic reasons, although three managers said that if the institutional framework in the UK deteriorated further in terms of government interference, taxation and labour problems they would be willing to shift production abroad. The institutional background apart, five firms intend to develop UK production and continue a strategy of penetrating overseas markets with exports. In offering an explanation for its UK production orientation, one firm stressed the highly skilled nature of the production process which has been developed by highly trained specialists over time. Another feels that the UK operation would lose production economies of scale. The costs of employing foreign labour in the host country militates against overseas manufacture in two cases, and of course, it is true that at the moment Britain is one of the low cost labour countries in the Western world.

Expansion of the first overseas sales subsidiary itself and subsequent overseas ventures in new host country markets are the two components of expansion that can be fed into an overall success index. (Another type of expansion would be the setting up of an overseas production unit, although had firms actually done this, their experiences would have been revealed in earlier chapters.) On these two components, all the overseas sales subsidiaries have met with success.

9.4 Overall success

The composite success variable combines the individual indicators analysed above: growth, the firm's own evaluation of performance, expansion and expansion plans, the confidence to undertake further foreign investments.* Using these parameters Table 9.7 presents a classification of the overall

Table 9.7 Success ratings

Label	Rating	Number of firms/subsidiaries
Totally successful	4	1
Very successful	3	5
Average success	2	1
Not successful	1	1
Failure	0	1
		9

degree of success. A total success rating is given to firms who performed well in each category; firms who failed in only one category are rated as 'very successful'. Failure to achieve each additional indicator loses a point on the overall success rating scale.

These success ratings will be used in the following sections as

---

*Consideration of the profitability of the overseas sales subsidiary has been omitted from the overall success index, in contrast to the treatment of the success of overseas production subsidiaries. The reason is that with the low-cost nature of an overseas sales subsidiary, profitability of the subsidiary can be altered by only marginal changes in transfer prices. Only three of the nine firms priced 'at arm's length'; the remainder, except for one firm which refused any answer on transfer prices, priced at levels which favoured the subsidiary.

an objective instrument to evaluate particular aspects of setting up and operating an overseas sales subsidiary.

9.5 Reasons for establishing an overseas sales subsidiary

Section 9.1 showed that six firms had previous experience of the host country market before they decided to set up an overseas sales subsidiary. Three firms had confined their sales efforts to the UK and had no previous experience of international markets to call upon. Why then did these firms change their marketing strategy and set up overseas sales subsidiaries? Motivations of course vary between firms and are often blurred within firms. Accordingly, firms were asked to give main and secondary motives which were then classified into 'pull' and 'push' categories as in the case of the setting up of an overseas production subsidiary.

Of the non-exporters, one firm explained its single most important motive in terms of a desire to expand sales in new markets. The sales outlet in Canada was set up 'to provide the firm with a springboard for attacking the larger and more important USA market'. On the basis of the factor classification described in Chapter 4, this is regarded as a market-induced pull. The other two ventures were based on push motives. One set up abroad to avoid the peaks and troughs of production which were caused by UK market conditions. The firm was therefore seeking overseas outlets to enable it to smooth out production schedules in the UK. The third non-exporter had a defensive motive. It faced severe competition from European rivals in the domestic UK market. Its response was to attack competitors in their home markets in order to increase UK exports at the expense of competitors' domestic sales. The firm adopted the strategy of 'attack is the best form of defence'; this rationale is classified here as a push motive, although it contains a large element of pull.

Of firms with previous exporting experience, customers'

needs were the single most important motivational factors in three cases. These are market-induced pull factors relating specifically to requirements in established export markets. By way of example, one firm was obliged to provide a follow-up servicing and maintenance function for products sold in France if it was to compete effectively with locally based competitors. A derived advantage found by this firm was that a local presence enabled them to keep ahead of competitors' product adaptation through their acquisition of knowledge about customers' tastes and requirements. Another firm whose rationale can be classified to customers' needs stressed the need of ensuring rapid delivery of products and eliminating the variables involved in direct delivery from the UK. Existing markets were the main impetus for the setting up of two other overseas sales subsidiaries. In one case the manager changed his overseas marketing strategy because he believed that direct representation in sales subsidiary form would produce 'better' results than the present agents in West Germany were achieving. The other market-induced specific pull investment was also in West Germany and occurred when the firm's main European competitor was acquired by an American multinational firm whose main activities were in non-competing lines. The UK firm set up and took over the former competitors' customers. The final venture was set up when the UK firm designed and developed a product which had no market in the UK — this is regarded as a push motive.

Table 9.8 summarises these responses and shows the main success ratings for the two groups ('pull' and 'push').

Secondary motives for establishing an overseas sales subsidiary are numerous. One firm felt that an overseas facility would enable it to approach foreign companies who are not equipped to deal with overseas (UK) suppliers. The most frequently cited secondary motives, however, were profit expectations ('pull') and spreading financial interests outside the UK ('push'), which some managers see as their only response to existing trends in the UK economy which are beyond their control. One firm designed its overseas selling system 'so as to keep any profits made out of the successively spendthrift Chancellors' maw, so that money so saved could be used to stimulate business and productive employment instead of strangling it'. (The reader is left to categorise this motive himself!)

Table 9.8

What was the single most important factor that led your firm to set up that first overseas subsidiary in . . . ?

	Number of firms	Mean success rating
Specific market-induced pull factors	6	3.0
Customers' needs		
Do a better job than agents		
Large market abroad		
Push factors	3	1.3
Smooth production profile		
No market in UK for new product		
Attack European competitors in their home markets		

The sample size, nine, is too small to reach conclusions as valid as those reached in connection with overseas production subsidiaries, but for overseas sales subsidiaries it does appear that, like the production subsidiaries, those established for market-based reasons are more likely to be successful than those established as a response to conditions in the UK.

9.6 Exporting experience

In Chapter 4 it was said that a firm contemplating overseas investment faces an uncertain situation with one particularly important scarce resource — information — and exporting experience is one means of providing the firm with the necessary information concerning the suitability of its products to market requirements. Exporting also enables firms to acquaint themselves with the host country environment and develop links and contacts which can be useful sources of additional information when the firm takes up overseas marketing on its own account. Such contacts are typically customers, agents, competitors, local businessmen and local politicians. Firms which lack exporting experience do not have these links and contacts to draw on.

Section 4.1 showed that firms with exporting experience had on average more success with their overseas production subsidiary than firms without such experience. It appears true also in the case of the success of overseas sales subsidiaries.

Table 9.9 Exporting experience

	Number of firms	Mean success rating
Firms with:		
Exporting experience	6	3.0
No previous exporting experience	3	1.3

As Table 9.9 shows, the non-exporters as a group fared badly in comparison with firms which had an exporting tradition. The mean success ratings of the two groups are 1.3 and 3.0 respectively. This does not mean that firms with no previous exporting experience should never set up overseas sales subsidiaries, or that an exporting tradition ensures success. It does suggest however that non-exporters are typically placed at a disadvantage because of their unfamiliarity with the host country market environment and that in the absence of this experience, desk research and personal visits to the overseas market assume great significance.

The length of exporting experience of the sample firms varied from eighteen months to almost one hundred years. Some firms exported on a regular basis, others responded to occasional and sporadic orders. These factors do not appear to be important in determining the overall success of the venture in comparison with exporting experience itself.

Direct selling and agency representation are the two forms

of exporting in the sample. Again, neither method appeared to offer advantage over the other and neither method was associated on average with a successful overseas sales subsidiary.

This section has examined the marketing strategy of the sample firms in the host country before they established an overseas sales subsidiary. Previous exporting experience appears to be an important influence on overall success in terms of its enhancement of the information and knowledge input. Firms with no previous exporting experience could make up this deficiency by other means, but exporting would appear to offer the safest route to a successful overseas sales subsidiary.

9.7 Preparation and entry

This section will deal with the equivalent of the planning and investing stages for the overseas production subsidiaries. While the commitment of capital is lower for the overseas sales subsidiary, the capital nevertheless needs to be spent as profitably as possible and hence some preparation and entry research and planning need to be done. None of the sample firms commissioned outside professionals to investigate overseas markets on their behalf. Most firms, however, did informal and internal market surveys. These comprised a mixture of sales representatives' reports and follow-up visits by at least one member of the UK board. Direct and indirect approaches to customers and competitors were made in several cases. One firm also had the co-operation of its agent, who became a partner in the new venture. In another case the overseas sales subsidiary sales director (-elect) lived in the host country for two years investigating the market in depth. This overseas sales subsidiary turned out as a total success, vindicating the expense of extensive market research before setting up the subsidiary. Another firm exhibited its products at an international industry exhibition and in response to promising demand and great interest in its products, set up an overseas sales subsidiary. However, orders did not materialise. The classic case of 'let's go do something in . . .' typifies the 'hunch' basis of decision making in another firm. Fortunately the 'hunch' was correct and the investment was successful. However it cannot be recommended that firms invest overseas on the basis of such vague criteria.

Smaller firms have limited resources, and for them to undertake sophisticated market appraisal is difficult and commissioning such work is expensive. However, general market indicators are readily and freely available from many sources. Statistics on per capita incomes, market size, cost of buildings and many other indicators of an economy, can be obtained in pamphlets freely available from host country embassies. (See Appendix I.) Managers contemplating overseas investment may be put in touch with others who have previously established operations abroad. A local partner may be useful. In some countries it is advisable, and even imperative, to have a local partner in order to tie someone down to act for the firm. In some cases joint ventures may be the only way of breaking into markets. But from the experiences of overseas production subsidiary firms, the advice must be to treat such approaches with caution, and to pick partners very carefully.

Preparation for entry is essential but what is the best form of entry? The answer is expected to emerge from information gathered in the planning stages and reflect the requirements and circumstances of the investing firm. No blanket recommendation of a best strategy can be made on the basis of the sample firms. However, the cheapest form of entry for setting up an overseas sales subsidiary is to form a new company registered in the host country. This strategy gives the firm freedom to scale commitment of resources to the host country market to its particular needs. Takeovers of marketing organisations are expensive in terms of goodwill, and firms inherit other products marketed by previous owners.

All sample firms agreed on this and indeed none had taken over an existing concern. Another method of minimising the initial investment outlay is to rent ready-built premises rather than buying facilities outright. This enables the market to be tested before greater commitment is made. Again all firms had in fact adopted this policy and one had already outgrown its leased facilities and had commissioned purpose-built accommodation.

Financial incentives from national, regional and local agencies are important in the siting decisions of firms setting up an overseas production subsidiary. Inducements vary from country to country, but generally are not available to firms setting up a sales subsidiary unless a building or employment programme is envisaged.

Once established, the overseas sales subsidiary can take on the marketing and distribution activities of other foreign firms, UK or otherwise, providing for them a form of agency representation in the host market. The advantage of having a wider product-mix is that product sales may affect each other in terms of rise and fall providing stability of income, and if adequate storage and distribution facilities are available, a greater volume of goods will ensure fuller utilisation of resources and economies of scale in warehousing and distribution. In the sample, only two firms acted as distributors for other firms in this way. Both were 'very successful' on the overall rating scale.

Analysis in this section has not been extensive, largely because preparation and entry by the sample firms were not extensive. However, the overall impression from the interviews must be that success, on average, flowed to the firms that worked for it.

9.8 Control

In order to make effective decisions, UK managers need to

know what is going on overseas. As in the case of the overseas production subsidiary, managers were asked the frequency at which they receive budget estimates and accounts, and sales forecasts and results from the subsidiary.

One UK parent adopted a local autonomy policy and receives an annual balance sheet from its subsidiary. In two cases accounts are received half-yearly and in another two cases they are received quarterly. Four subsidiaries report monthly. None of the firms utilises budget estimates for their overseas units, but all except the autonomous unit provide monthly or quarterly forecasts of likely sales in the year ahead.

In addition managers were asked the location of responsibility for a range of functions. Four overseas sales subsidiaries' management boards have complete discretion in changing prices, wages and levels of advertising expenditure. Of the remainder, four are required to seek permission to increase wages and advertising expenditure, and one firm has to obtain approval for increasing prices.

Similarly the range of spending that the local board can authorise varies markedly. No upper limit has been set in three cases, but UK directors are also members of the local board, and so ensure that spending and other policy decisions are in line with group policy. Of the remaining firms, £1000 was the maximum expenditure allowed without special permission in two cases; £500 was set in two others, £100 in another, and 'anything beyond routine spending' has to be approved in another. Upper spending limits appear to be important control mechanisms particularly when host country legislation requires a majority of nationals on the local board.

An overseas subsidiary by virtue of distance is more difficult to control than a UK subsidiary, particularly if the UK parent relies on a 'personalised' style of managerial control. A manager cannot be making daily trips abroad to check on what local management is doing. Managers of all of the sample group of firms felt that they control the overseas sales subsidiaries more leniently than they do UK subsidiaries. Distance was the single most important factor cited to account for this. Additionally, one firm feels that the small scale of operation and the fact that the overseas sales subsidiary is successful accounts for its more relaxed attitude. Another firm's non-intervention policy arises from its belief that local management knows local conditions and that UK supervision would only duplicate the work load. Again, perhaps the lower amounts of capital at stake in an overseas sales subsidiary mean that more lenient control can be experimented with and maintained until problems arise.

Either gained from textbooks, or from folklore, there is a widespread belief that it is necessary to maintain higher levels of stock overseas than in the UK to avoid shortages that may arise from an inability to supply for one of very many different reasons, which may or may not be in-company. The experiences of the firms in the sample refute this. All keep lower stock holdings overseas than in the UK in terms of a stocks/weeks-sales ratio. This ratio varies from four to twenty-five weeks between the sample group of firms (depending on the product) but in all cases it was lower than the ratio in the UK.

In the case of overseas production subsidiaries, there was a conflict between those firms who believed that it is essential to recruit a local national as chief executive and those who thought that at all costs the chief executive must be British. In the case of overseas sales subsidiaries, the picture of two conflicting schools of thought is again prevalent. In five cases a local national is in charge of the subsidiary; in four, a Briton. Similarly four firms sent out UK personnel to fill the senior management positions in the overseas sales subsidiary when it was established, and five firms recruited local nationals. The 'four' and 'five' firms are not the same in both cases. The overseas sales subsidiary which rates as 'a total success' is run by nationals of the host country, whereas the investment classified as 'a complete failure' has a British senior management team led by a British chief executive. This does not mean that local managers will succeed and British expatriates will fail and on average there is no difference in success between the two groups but again the essential factor is that the 'right' man is chosen as chief executive in the particular circumstances faced by the firm.

In respect of control procedures, leniency appeared to be normal for the nine sample firms in their dealing with their overseas sales subsidiaries and consequently comparisons of different methods or degrees of control cannot be made. There seemed little doubt however that the leniency extends only as long as the subsidiary is successful. In a sense this is an unfair policy for a head office to adopt. It does encourage local initiative but head office is in effect saying that it wants no responsibility for any decisions other than successful ones.

Executive summary

This chapter has described the experiences of a small sample of firms in setting up sales subsidiaries overseas for the first time. The analysis has followed closely upon the lines developed in earlier chapters for the establishment of an overseas production unit. A composite yardstick of success was built and used to evaluate the merits of firms' rationale and decision-making.

The first sections were concerned with measuring success and the normal range of outcomes from totally successful through to failure was found in the sample. Not found were the disastrous failures that occurred in the sample of overseas production subsidiaries. The reason for this, and the reason underlies much of the comment in this chapter, is that an overseas sales subsidiary is a much lower level of commitment than an overseas production subsidiary. The capital consigned is lower and while revenues are equally uncontrollable for either subsidiary, the costs of operating an overseas sales subsidiary are much lower and have a significantly higher proportion of variable costs which means overall costs can be adjusted to suit revenue.

Section 9.5 gave the reasons why the firms opened their first overseas sales subsidiaries. The reasons showed wide variation but in spite of the small sample size success, on average, was higher for the firms which gave some positive attraction of the foreign market as the reason, compared with the firms which, for one reason or another, felt some desire to go beyond solely-UK operations. This finding is the same as that for overseas production subsidiaries.

Exporting experience is one way of gaining knowledge about conditions, customs and ethics in a foreign country. The firms which had exported to the country in which they founded their first overseas sales subsidiary had higher mean success ratings than the firms which went overseas without exporting experience. This conclusion, in Section 9.6, is consistent with the higher success going to those overseas production subsidiaries which proceeded step-by-step rather than directly from just UK experience.

In Section 9.7 preparation and entry by the sample firms was commented upon. However, perhaps the main conclusion is that preparation for entry was not extensive. All the firms entered by setting up companies and leasing premises; there was no entry by takeover.

In terms of control procedures in Section 9.8, the main comment must be that control procedures were not extensive; local autonomy was the usual policy.

An overseas sales subsidiary is not automatically successful in generating increased sales. If the market is limited, uncertain or risky, firms may find agency representation or direct selling more appropriate. However, where there is a proven market, which is growing, an overseas sales subsidiary, which is one step upwards in terms of riskiness and commitment, appears to generate sales which more than compensate for the extra risk. For those firms considering setting up an overseas sales subsidiary, many of the comments made in earlier chapters about the setting up of overseas production subsidiaries would be useful supplements to this chapter and should lead to greater success.

10 Profile of a successful production subsidiary

Accepting the danger that a simplified summary may enhance some factors at the expense of others, this chapter simply lists those factors from preceding chapters which appear to be part of a successful overseas production subsidiary. The listing is provided so as to enable managers to compare quickly their own subsidiaries, or their own plans, with the profile of the successful subsidiary built up from this report. The list should not be taken separately from the comments made in the body of the report. A successful overseas production subsidiary appears to be:

(1) the fourth or fifth step in the process of going international (Section 4.1);
(2) based upon substantial export experience (Section 4.1);
(3) not founded in response to an outside stimulus (Section 4.2);
(4) not founded in response to conditions in the UK (Section 4.3);
(5) founded in response to host country market factors (Section 4.3);

(6) located in a country where conditions have proved to be conducive to the success of smaller UK firms (Section 4.5);
(7) is at least seventy-five per cent owned by the UK parent (Section 5.1);
(8) founded only after additional information on the host country has been gathered (Section 5.4);
(9) located where the main competition is from other UK subsidiaries (Section 5.4);
(10) founded only after additional information on the market has been gathered (Section 5.5);
(11) founded only after more than one executive made more than one trip to the host country (Section 5.6);
(12) selling products aimed at the market segment identical to that in the UK (Sections 6.1 and 6.2);
(13) has clear and multiple objectives laid down (Section 6.3);
(14) has clear financial targets set (Section 6.3);
(15) located on a site chosen for economic rather than historical or personal reasons (Section 6.4);
(16) has investigated host country inducements but not necessarily taken them up (Section 6.5);
(17) submitting monthly accounts (Section 7.1);
(18) submitting regular budget estimates (Section 7.1);
(19) realistically restricted in the capital expenditure it can make without UK authorisation (Section 7.1);
(20) autonomous within the guidelines of (17), (18), and (19) (Section 7.2);
(21) doing some research and development of its own (Section 7.2);
(22) at least as strictly controlled as UK subsidiaries (Section 7.3);
(23) run by a chief executive chosen on grounds of ability, not nationality (Section 7.4);
(24) able to give confidence in building an international strategy (Section 8.2);
(25) available to all sizes of firms (Section 8.3);
(26) available to all types of ownership of firms (Section 8.3).

In the analyses that have preceded this profile, it has been shown clearly that where managers took steps, which were sensible and realistic for the firm of the size they manage, to reduce the riskiness of the move overseas, the subsidiary was more successful than if less care had been taken.

For those managers which did take some care to reduce the risk, the rewards both in money and in personal accomplishment were large, and of the two rewards perhaps the most satisfying to those managers in the survey was the knowledge that they had taken their small firm overseas and beaten the competition in its own markets. *They* had made their firm international and successful.

It was well-known before this report that the managers of the BPs, the ICIs and other giants of the corporate world could go international and be successful. What the men named in the acknowledgements to the book have proved is that smaller firms can do it successfully and they have provided their experiences in this report to encourage and guide other smaller firms to follow them in going international.

Appendix I Regulations, policies and inducements, by country

This addendum will assist managers contemplating overseas investment in any of the many countries covered by the study. It provides information which will short-circuit an otherwise lengthy search for accurate information and assistance. This information and assistance is helpful and essential, but it is not a substitute for all desk research or a substitute for personal visits to a country. It is usually foolish, as shown in the study, to commit capital overseas without *thorough* investigation. Thus, the value of this addendum is in providing an overview of investment policies, in quickly identifying sources which managers can approach for further details and as a prelude to additional desk research and personal visits.

Each country has a different view on the value of inward foreign investment. Hence, often, permission from official bodies has to be sought before any stage of the investment can be carried out. In those countries where it is necessary to obtain permission, the result is a lengthening of the period between a decision being taken and its implementation.

In many countries, whether or not they are ones which require permission to invest, financial assistance to companies is offered. Usually, the assistance is part of the host government's regional and development strategy and is normally

Regulations, policies and inducements, by country

available to both foreign and domestic firms without prejudice. The scale of inducements has increased in recent years as countries compete with each other to attract new investment into their less prosperous areas and firms are recommended to investigate the possibilities and opportunities afforded by financial inducements. The investigation, as usual, needs care because inducements to invest in a particular area are offered only when good reasons exist, and each firm must decide whether the inducements are sufficient to overcome difficulties due to remoteness, bad environment, or lack of infrastructure. In the summary of countries' policies, the incentives with regard to particular regions have not been given in detail because of the volume of detail. The sources shown will supply detailed and up-to-date information.

Information was collected on each of the countries in which this study or official statistics showed investment from the UK took place. In the following pages there is listed for each country:

(1) The address of the contact ministry in the country and, where appropriate, the address of the UK representative of that ministry.

(2) The prerequisites and formalities of investing in the country—the need to obtain approval of investment intentions and rules and regulations regarding the transfer of capital and profits.

(3) The inducements or penalties to foreign investors arising from regional and development policies.

(4) Official publications on investing in the country.

Managers contemplating investment in any one of these coktries are advised to approach the relevant contact ministry direct for further details.

Countries are included in this appendix if the contact ministry has read the entry below and has approved it as a summary; when the contact ministry was unwilling to approve the entry or supply one in its place, the country has been omitted since there is no verification that the details truly reflect current views and policies.

Australia

Contact ministry

The Executive Member
Foreign Investment Review
Board
c/o The Treasury
Parkes Place
Canberra ACT 2600
Australia

Reserve Bank of Australia
65 Martin Place
Sydney NSW 2000
Australia

in the UK:

Minister (Financial)
Australian High Commission
Australia House
The Strand
London WC2B 4LA

Office of the Trade
Commissioner
Overseas Trade Office
Australia House
The Strand
London WC2B 4LA

Formalities

(a) Foreign investment policy. Certain foreign investment proposals require Australian Government approval before they can be implemented. Such proposals — see below — are examined by the Foreign Investment Review Board against the background of the Government's basic aim of encouraging foreign investment while ensuring that there is a fair sharing of the net benefits as between the foreign investor and the Australian people.

Examinable foreign investment proposals include:
— all takeovers of existing Australian businesses;
— all proposals involving the establishment of a new non-bank

financial institution or insurance company;
—proposals for the establishment of other new businesses where an investment of $A1 million or more in any 12 months period is involved;
—certain real estate acquisitions.

The main criteria used by the Foreign Investment Review Board in examining the above investment proposals include the extent of Australian ownership and control and the net economic benefits accruing to Australia from the investment. The latter include such things as: the effect on the industrial base and productive capacity; the introduction of new technology, managerial skills and other know-how; the development of new markets; competition and efficiency; employment; and quality and range of products and services made available. There are no specific rules relating to Australian equity participation except those relating to natural resource projects in areas such as mining, forestry, farming and fishing. In these areas a 50% Australian involvement is required, although, if such Australian participation is unavailable, the Government will not prevent an otherwise acceptable proposal from proceeding. In the field of uranium production there is a strict requirement for 75% Australian equity and Australian control.

Takeover proposals must by law be decided within a maximum period of 140 days and applicants in the non-takeover areas can expect to receive a decision within a maximum of 90 days. In practice, most proposals are decided in a substantially shorter period.

(b) Exchange control. Exchange control in Australia is administered by the Reserve Bank of Australia on behalf of the Government. Authority is required for the buying and selling of foreign currency, for all internal payments on non-resident account and for contracts (other than contracts for the purchase of goods) with non-residents. Authority is also required for Australian residents to borrow from non-residents or to allot, transfer or send securities to them. For exchange

control purposes, individuals ordinarily resident in Australia and companies incorporated in Australia are residents. In addition, foreign companies having a place of business in Australia are deemed to be Australian residents in relation to their Australian affairs.

Overseas firms proposing to establish a business in Australia or enter into contracts or agreements with Australian residents need therefore to ensure that the necessary Reserve Bank exchange control authorities have been obtained.

There are some requirements in relation to the periods within which certain current transactions may be settled but, apart from these, generally no restrictions are placed on the receipt or remittance of funds for settlement of such transactions. For example, payments for imports must be made within six months after arrival of goods; interest and dividend payments (after taxation) due to non-residents must be paid not later than one month after becoming contractually due.

Exchange control approval is normally readily forthcoming for the remission overseas of all current net income (after taxation) accruing to non-residents. Approval for repatriation of capital is normally readily granted, provided there is evidence of the inward transfer, but no advance commitments are given. Transfers of capital would, if the transfer was to a tax haven, be subject to screening by the Australian taxation office to check avoidance or evasion of Australian tax. Without approval by the taxation office, exchange control approval for transmission of funds cannot be obtained.

Regional industrialisation incentives

There are no inducements specifically available for persons contemplating investment in Australia, although a number of inducements exist for Australian industry in which the newly established foreign-owned industry may participate. These include an investment allowance under which, in addition to normal depreciation, a deduction of a specified percentage of the cost of plant and equipment is allowed in the year in which the plant and equipment is first used or installed ready for use. The percentage rates are 40% for plant ordered and installed between 1 Jan 1976 and 30 June 1978; and 20% for the period 1 July 1978 to 30 June 1983. Special tax provisions apply to the mining and petroleum industries and it should also be noted that Australia has a double taxation agreement with the UK. For current information on regional industry locating incentives that may exist it is suggested that enquiries be made to the relevant State Agent-General in London.

Official publications

Australia & New Zealand (ANZ) Bank publications: *Establishment of Industry in Australia*; *Business Formation in Australia: Legal and Taxation Implications*. Copies available on request.

A number of other official publications useful to the potential investor are available from the Office of the Minister (Financial) at Australia House, London.

Belgium

Contact ministry

Ministry of Economic Affairs
Service for Economic Expansion and Foreign Investment
15–17 Belliardstreet
1040 Brussels
Belgium

in the UK:
Economic Section
Ambassade de Belgique
103 Eaton Square
London SW1W 9AB

Formalities

Transfers of capital into the Belgo-Luxembourg Economic

Union can be made freely through the 'free' and 'official' exchange markets. Capital transfers from Belgium are made through the 'free' exchange market. At the time of investment, the exchange control authorities give an assurance that permission to transfer the proceeds and income from the investment will be granted at any time. This follows approval of the project by the Belgo-Luxembourg exchange institute which fixes the terms and conditions under which payments and transfers of goods between the Belgo-Luxembourg Economic Union and other countries should be made. Special licences are only required when proposed transfers are not generally approved by the regulations.

Freedom of establishment — any foreign firm can set up in Belgium without special authorisation, whether as a subsidiary or a branch of a company incorporated in another country. A foreign company has the same rights and obligations as Belgian companies. Formalities are: Act of Incorporation, Balance Sheet, Address of Registered Office, Commercial Register number.

Foreign investors in Belgium should contact the special service for foreign investment for particular advice on the formation of a subsidiary, its corporate charter, indirect taxes, employment and labor conditions, social security, work permit and professional card regulations, credit terms and technical questions about new plant location.

Regional industrialisation incentives

By the laws of July 1959 and December 1970, the authorities sponsor and promote industrial and economic development. Investing firms, both Belgian and foreign, are offered assistance, depending upon the nature and location of the proposed investment. The principal forms of assistance are:

1. Interest rate subsidies.
2. Capital investment grants.
3. Employment premiums and training subsidies.

4. Exemption from provincial and commune taxes for up to five years.
5. Government guarantees in respect of principal and interest on loans.
6. Accelerated depreciation of plant and machinery on either a straight line or degressive system.
7. Favourable treatment for the purposes of income tax assessment of foreign managers and employees of foreign firms, regarding such people as non-residents although they may reside in Belgium for a certain period of time.

Official publications

Promotion of Foreign Investments in Belgium (May 1976) published by the Ministry of Economic Affairs; *Taxation of Income in Belgium* (December 1975); *Belgium — Investment Guide*.

Canada

Contact ministry

Foreign Investment Review Agency
Ottawa
Canada KIP 6A5

in the UK:
Commercial Division
Canadian High Commission
1 Grosvenor Square
London W1X 0AB

Formalities

Firms proposing to invest in Canada are advised to contact the Commercial Division of the Canadian High Commission in London before formal application to invest in Canada is made to the Foreign Investment Review Agency. Once approval is obtained, a subsidiary company may be established either federally or under the laws of one of the ten provinces. Firms intending to carry on business throughout Canada are obliged

Appendix I

to obtain a further licence to trade in some provinces, although firms conducting specialised service activities are covered by special Acts of Provincial and Federal Parliaments.

Regional industrialisation incentives

Financial incentives for new investment are administered federally through the Department of Regional Economic Expansion, to whom application for assistance should be made as soon as the Foreign Investment Review Agency approves the proposed investment. Financial assistance varies from area to area, but it is most generous in the Atlantic region comprising Newfoundland, Nova Scotia, Prince Edward Island and New Brunswick. Other designated areas, including most of Quebec and Northern Ontario, qualify for proportionally less in terms of the grant payable as a fixed percentage of one year's wages and salaries bill averaged over the second and third years of operation. In the Atlantic region this percentage is 30%.

Other financial incentives include:

1. Grants for new investments of up to 25% of the cost of eligible assets.
2. A grant of 20% of the cost of eligible assets for investments comprising modernisations and volume expansions.

Each of the Provincial Governments offers a further package of pecuniary and non-pecuniary benefits to firms who locate investments in their territory.

Official publications

Doing Business in Canada; *Information Kit on the Foreign Investment Review Agency*; *Information Kit on the Department of Region Economic Expansion.*

All the above are available from the Commercial Division of the Canadian High Commission on request. Location decisions within Canada may be helped by consulting the wide range of pamphlets and brochures issued by each of the provincial authorities.

France

Contact ministry

Ministere de l'Economie et
des Finances:
Direction du Tresor
42 rue de Clichy
75009 Paris

Delegation a l'Amenagement
du Territoire et a l'Action
Regionale (DATAR)*
Director: Jerome Monod
1 Avenue Charles-Floquet
75007 Paris

in the UK:
French Industrial
Development Board
Adviser: Philippe Girbal
12 Stanhope Gate
London W1Y 6JH

Formalities

Firms wishing to set up an office or subsidiary in France must first obtain specific approval of the Ministry of Economy and Finance. This is also required in cases where firms propose to acquire or increase their measure of control over a French company. The Ministry also exercises control over loans made between French non-resident controlled companies and over guarantees given by non-residents. The disposal of investments by non-resident companies is free but transfers abroad have to be authorised if they exceed one million French francs. Remittance of profits and dividends, as well as payments for royalties and patents can be made freely to the UK.

---

*Industrial Development Board.

Appendix I

Regional industrialisation incentives

These apply equally to both French and foreign-owned operations. Their purpose is to achieve balanced regional development through France and prevent further concentration in the Paris and Lyons regions. Investment incentives apply in all areas except the Paris and Lyons areas, although the scale of inducement varies in line with the 'attractiveness' of the area. A special tax is raised on firms taking up industrial facilities and office space in the Paris region. Applications for a regional development grant should be lodged with the Prefecture of the region where investment is intended before any part of the proposed investment is made. It is also necessary to obtain a building permit in advance if the construction of new buildings is intended; this is also obtained from the regional Prefecture.

The investment incentives, where applicable, comprise:

1. A cash grant, payable over 2–3 years, of up to 25% of the amount invested in industrial activities and scientific or technical research and development establishments excluding investments in agriculture and food processing.
2. A cash grant, payable over 2–3 years, of up to 20% of the amount invested in non-industrial facilities in areas where the regional development grant applies and also in selected metropolitan areas outside the Paris and Lyons regions.
3. A decentralisation indemnity equal to a percentage of the transfer costs is available to firms who relocate their activities outside the Paris Basin area, providing that they vacate at least 500 square metres of industrial premises in that area.
4. Tax relief measures are available in several forms: (a) exemption in whole or in part from the local business tax for up to 5 years; (b) reduction of transfer taxes on the purchase of a business or plant more than 5 years old; (c) accelerated depreciation of construction costs including an immediate 25% depreciation of costs upon completion of a construction; (d) reduction of the capital gains tax on land.
5. Subsidies for job training.

6. Subsidies for personnel moving and relocation expenses.

Official publications
Published by the DATAR: *Foreign Investment and Regional Planning in France*; *Investment Incentives in France*.

Ireland

Contact ministry

Industrial Development
Authority (IDA)
Head Office
Lansdowne House
Dublin 4

in the UK:
IDA – Ireland
Director: Hugh Alston
28 Bruton Street
London W1X 7DB

Formalities

As Ireland is part of the Sterling Area, there are no exchange controls on transactions or investments between Ireland and the UK. Firms of other nationalities proposing to invest in Ireland require the approval of the Central Bank.

The submission of industrial proposals should be made through the Industrial Development Authority which is the state sponsored agency responsible for attracting investments and administering the package of incentives offered to investors.

Regional industrialisation incentives

Since 1971 Ireland has offered a wide range of incentives, the most important of which are:

1. A cash grant of up to 50% of the costs of investment in land, buildings and machinery. The general level of capital grant aid is about 35% of the costs of investment depending

on area and the rating of benefits that the proposed investment will bring to the economy.
2. Ready or purpose-built factory accommodation on large industrial sites is available as well as advance factories at many locations throughout the country.
3. Profits from sales of goods exported up to 1990 are exempt from taxation.
4. Grants for personnel training in conjunction with AnCO — the Industrial Training Authority — are available.

Official publications

A multiplicity of pamphlets and booklets are available from the IDA on request.

Luxembourg

Contact ministry

Ministry of National Economy
19 Bd. Royal
Luxembourg
Grand Duchy of Luxembourg

in the UK:
Luxembourg Embassy in London
Commercial Division
27 Wilton Crescent
London SW1X 8SD

Formalities

A government permit is required before any commercial or industrial enterprise can establish operations in Luxembourg. This is obtained from the Ministry of National Economy on payment of a 500 Fr. setting-up fee. Within one month of commencing operations, the subsidiary must be registered with the record office of the *Tribune de Commerce*, Palais de Justice, Luxembourg, and the articles of association published in the official journal *Memorial*. Registration can only be made upon presentation of the government permit to establish. The transfer of capital is made freely through the official and free currency markets. At the time of investment the government guarantees the free transfer or repatriation of capital and dividends.

Regional industrialisation incentives

Firms contributing to the improvement of the general structure or regional balance of the economy are eligible for substantial temporary tax reliefs and other forms of financial assistance. There is no distinction in the availability of such benefits to foreign or Luxembourg investors. Each investment project is evaluated on its merits to discern the size and nature of assistance that the authorities are willing to make available to companies. The main incentive facilities comprise:

1. The making available of land for industrial development.
2. Government guarantees of loans negotiated from credit institutions with regard to the repayment of principal and interest (exceptionally).
3. Interest rate subsidies of 2.5% for an initial period of 5 years on investment loans negotiated from authorised credit institutions.
4. Capital grants not exceeding 15% (generally about 10% of the total investment in plant and machinery.
5. Training subsidies.
6. Tax relief: (i) accelerated depreciation of assets on a degressive basis; (ii) a 25% exemption of taxable profits from Corporation Income Tax (State Tax) and Business Tax (Municipal Tax) for the first 8 years of operations but advantage limited to a fraction of fixed investment to be determined for each project.
7. Investment tax credits: a tax credit which offsets taxes otherwise payable on income is granted in respect of investments in movable fixed assets carried out during a given fiscal year; (credit is subject to expiry and renewal, therefore check with the Embassy in London).

Appendix I

Official publications

Papers are available from the Luxembourg Embassy on all aspects of investment in Luxembourg, on request.

The Netherlands

Contact ministry

Industrial Projects Division of the Ministry of Economic Affairs
The Director
Bezuidenhoutseweg 30
The Hague

in the UK:
Economic Department
Royal Netherlands Embassy
34 Hyde Park Gate
London SW7 5DP

Formalities

Firms intending to establish a subsidiary in the Netherlands must obtain an exchange licence issued by the Netherlands Bank (*De Nederlandsche Bank NV*). This is obtained after approval for the project is given by the Industrial Projects Division of the Ministry of Economic Affairs. For this it is important to supply the division with the fullest possible information about the nature and size of the project. Once approval is given, application can be made through a Bank for the exchange licence which entitles the firm automatically to all available benefits regarding the free transfer of profits and the retransfer of capital. Industrial projects are required to comply with the environmental hygiene laws — Pollution of Surface Waters Act, the Air Pollution Act and the Public Nuisance Act. Firms who are liable to cause danger, damage or nuisance to their surroundings must obtain a licence from the Mayor and Aldermen of the municipality in which they intend to site the investment.

Regional industrialisation incentives

These apply equally to Dutch and foreign-owned operations. Financial incentives in several forms are available to firms settling *outside* the western part of the country:

1. An investment premium representing up to 25% of the capital expenditure on fixed assets is payable to firms establishing or expanding industrial enterprises up to a maximum of FL3 500 000.

Alternatively a mixed premium not exceeding FL4 000 000 is available to investors. This comprises a premium of 15% of the capital expenditure on fixed assets, plus a grant of FL10 000 for each permanent job created as a direct consequence of the new investment.

2. Projects considered to be particularly valuable to an area's economy may be eligible for interest subsidies for the establishment of new industrial enterprises up to a maximum of 3% per annum over a period not exceeding 15 years.

3. In certain cases it is possible to obtain long-term loans from the National Investment Bank (*Nationale Inversterings Bank*), principal and interest guaranteed by the state.

4. Tax incentives: (a) one third of the cost of acquisition of buildings can be written off at an accelerated rate in all areas except the West; (b) new enterprises are allowed to offset losses made in the first 6 years against later profits for an unlimited period.

5. Training subsidies are available to compensate trainees for the loss of earnings during the training period. Also the curriculum of a centre for vocational training can be adapted to the particular requirements of a specific company.

Inside the Western Region: Increasing concentration of industry and population has led to attempts to check further development through the Selective Investment Act (1972) in this region. Included in the law is a system of levies and permits plus a compulsory notification system aimed at curbing the establishment and expansion of companies in the

Appendix I

Western Region. The 25% levy on buildings and 3% levy on installations have been recently suspended and the whole system is now under review. The permit system is still in operation. It is forbidden to construct buildings and installations without first acquiring a permit. Considerations such as the concentration of industry and population as well as the economic structure or the labour market position are made before the permit is granted. The compulsory notification system requires that the Ministry of Economic Affairs be informed of all intentions to build at least one month before commencement in order to judge the desirability of the proposed investment and whether or not to issue a permit.

Official publications

The Netherlands: Basic Guide to Establishing Industrial Operations, published by the Ministry of Economic Affairs.

New Zealand

Contact ministry

The Secretary
Overseas Investment Commission
c/o Reserve Bank of New Zealand
PO Box 2498
Wellington
New Zealand

Formalities

Before firms can commence operations or incorporate a subsidiary in New Zealand, it is necessary to obtain permission from the Overseas Investment Commission. If it is intended to acquire control of 25% or more of a New Zealand company, the consent of the Commission must first be obtained. No restrictions are placed on capital transfers to New Zealand made through approved channels. Remittances of interest, profit and dividends can be made freely provided the prior approval of the Reserve Bank is obtained, and that such payments are authenticated by an auditor's certificate or in other approved manners. Repatriation of capital is allowed, providing that such capital was originally transferred to New Zealand through approved channels. However, in cases where investment is made in the form of goods imported to New Zealand without corresponding payment overseas, repatriation of capital is not normally allowed unless the Customs Department would have been prepared to issue a remitting import licence in the first place. A certificate to this effect should be obtained from the Customs Department at the time of investment.

Foreign investors are expected to finance investment largely from overseas sources in order to supplement local capital resources. Foreign investors wishing to raise or borrow money in New Zealand require the prior approval of the Commission; the general rule is that foreign-owned or controlled companies may raise loan capital in New Zealand assessed partly on turnover and partly on the proportion of equity capital owned by New Zealand residents. There are no fixed rules requiring a minimum proportion of equity to be held by New Zealand residents, but local participation and involvement is preferred.

Payments and transfers in respect of know-how, trade markets, patents or other assets require the approval of the Reserve Bank of New Zealand.

Application must be made to the Registrar of Companies for approval of a proposed name; this should be renewed every three months as there exists no provision for the reservation of a name.

Building projects require the prior approval of the relevant local authority and need to conform with the requirements of environmental and town planning provisions.

Regional industrialisation incentives

New Zealand encourages the development of industries with high export potential and offers tax incentives to exporters. Further details of incentives can be obtained from:

Department of Trade and Industry
Private Bag
Wellington
New Zealand

Official publications

Investment in New Zealand by Overseas Residents (a booklet prepared by the Overseas Investment Commission in conjunction with the Reserve Bank of New Zealand).

Norway

Contact ministry

Royal Ministry of Industry and Handicraft
Box 8014 Department
Oslo 1
Norway

The Regional Development Fund
Box 8165 Department
Oslo 1
Norway

in the UK:
Royal Norwegian Embassy
Commercial Division
20 Pall Mall
London SW1

Formalities

Firms proposing to establish production facilities in Norway must make formal application for Concession under the terms of Concession Laws, which, *inter alia*, aim to regulate the activities in line with the policies of Norwegian government.

Informal contact with the Ministry of Industry and Handicraft should precede formal application. It is an accepted practice that where a foreign enterprise owns more than 10% of the share capital of a Norwegian firm, there must be a Norwegian majority on the board of directors and the trading licence must be in the possession of a Norwegian director. This condition holds regardless of the type of organisation or legal identity used by the subsidiary.

Other standard conditions for the establishment of wholly or partially owned foreign enterprises include a requirement that a specified proportion of share capital must be Norwegian, that transfers between the foreign firm and its Norwegian subsidiary are based on a realistic pricing policy approved by the Ministry of Industry in addition to the requirement that all agreements regarding payment for economic, technical, mercantile and all other forms of assistance be approved. These standard requirements are often supplemented by special concession conditions which vary from company to company, namely ownership arrangements, financing and capitalisation terms, degree of processing and geographical location. Foreign firms are not allowed to acquire forests for forestry operations and concessions for the acquisition of waterfalls are only granted under exceptional circumstances.

In only minor cases can the Ministry give an independent decision on the proposed investment; normally the Ministry initiates an evaluation process which involves submitting the application to municipal and country authorities, and other interested parties, for example, cases involving the development or leasing of hydroelectric power are submitted to the Norwegian Water Resources and Electricity Board.

Foreign exchange transfers must be made at rates established by the Bank of Norway.

Regional industrialisation incentives

Government regional policy of developing and strengthening

existing industry as well as stimulating the establishment of new enterprises is carried out through the Regional Development Fund supplemented by Country Development Agencies. The Fund encourages investment projects which provide increased, permanent and viable job opportunities in areas with special employment problems or having a poorly developed economic base. To this end, the fund offers would-be investors various forms of financial incentives:

1. Granting of loans and guaranteeing of loans negotiated through banking channels.
2. In special cases, the Fund subscribes to stock on its own account.
3. In some cases, the Fund contributes to the cost of planning and research not firectly related to concrete projects.
4. Financial assistance is given towards removal expenses and the costs of special training of manpower.

Official publications

Regional Development in Norway published by Regional Development Fund; *Establishing a Business in Norway: A Brief Guide For Foreign Firms* published by Kreditkassen (clearing bank).

South Africa

Contact ministry

Department of Industries
Private Bag X342
Pretoria
South Africa

in the UK:
Commercial Section
South African Embassy
Trafalgar Square
London WC2N 5DP

Formalities

It is necessary to decide whether to establish a locally incorporated subsidiary in South Africa or to conduct operations through a local branch. The main disadvantage of the latter form of organisation is that the annual capital duty is levied on the entire capital of the parent company compared with an annual levy on the subsidiary's capital. There are no restrictions on the inward transfer of funds through banking channels from the exchange control viewpoint, but as a general rule, the local sale proceeds of all non-resident owned investments are subject to the blocking procedure. This policy effectively delays the transfer of funds into foreign currency for 5 years. During this time the funds are placed in blocked accounts, but are eligible for reinvestment in locally quoted securities or Non-Resident Bonds issued by the Government, but only investment in the latter group of securities entitles the holder to foreign currency after 5 years. On the other hand, there are no restrictions on the transfer of dividends on current profits provided that such transfers are financed from cash resources available to the subsidiary. Prior approval of the exchange control authorities is needed for other permissible transfers, namely, royalty payments and technical service and management fees. As a general rule a non-resident owned subsidiary is only allowed to borrow 25% of the effective foreign capital invested in South Africa. This limit is increased by the ratio of local to foreign participation in cases where South African residents are allowed to own equity in the subsidiary.

South Africa follows a conscious and deliberate policy of tariff protection designed to encourage industrial development. Firms considering local manufacture in South Africa should make representations regarding the measure of protection required before they go ahead with the proposed investment.

Regional industrialisation incentives

These apply mainly to recognised economic growth centres and the Bantu Homelands. In the latter areas, special homelands' institutions have been established to develop and supply infrastructural needs of industrial enterprises setting up in their territories. In South Africa itself, the authorities are keen to decentralise the expansion of industry away from the Pretoria-Witwatersrand-Vereeniging-Sasolburg complex. By applying an employment ratio of white : black employees, under the terms of the Environment Planning Act of 1967, the expansion and establishment of new factories in the area of concentration has been effectively curtailed. The Industrial Development Corporation is the main instrument for channelling assistance to firms. In the growth areas buildings are available on long leases at very low rates of interest. Housing for 'white' employees is also provided in the growth areas by the Industrial Development Corporation and the institutions of the 'homelands' governments.

Official publications

South Africa 1975, compiled and published by the South African Department of Information.

Sweden

Contact ministry

Kommerskollegium
(The Board of Trade)
Birger Jarlstorg 5
Box 1209
111 82 Stockholm

Sveriges Riksbank
(The Bank of Sweden)
Brunkebergstrog 11
Box 16283
103 25 Stockholm

Arbetsmarknadsstyrelsen AMS*
Sundbybergsvagen 9
171 99 Solna
(for regional incentives)

---

*The Labour Market Board.

Formalities

Firms proposing to establish a limited company in Sweden must first obtain the permission of the Bank of Sweden. Applications for permits to invest are normally approved. Thereafter profits, dividends and the sales proceeds of liquidating investments can be freely transferred or repatriated. The amount of the minimum share capital is 50 000 krona. Foreign nationals may only represent one third of the board of directors. In special cases the Board of Trade allows a foreign national to be managing director or to hold signing powers. The restrictions on the acquisition of real estate by foreign-owned or controlled firms are interpreted liberally for purposes of buying a house, factory, or industrial premises; but only in exceptional cases are such given permission to acquire forests, mines, waterfalls and agricultural property. Firms with more than 25 employees are required to permit worker representation in the form of two directors on the main board. Firms also have to observe governmental counter-cyclical policies particularly with regard to the investment reserve fund.

Regional industrialisation incentives

These incentives offered by the state apply equally to Swedish and foreign domiciled firms who locate their investments in the support area as defined in the Swedish Law 1976 no. 379. The scale of financial assistance offered by the local authority (*Kommun*) varies from one area to another. The system of planning permission is highly developed, requiring that a permit be obtained from the *Kommun* before any part of the proposed investment is made. Large projects may involve the state economic planning unit and the environmental protection council.

Official publications

Pamphlets and booklets can be obtained freely from the Board of Trade (*Kommerskollegium*).

USA

Contact ministry

The Office of Export Development
Bureau of International Commerce
Department of Commerce
Washington DC 20230

in the UK:
The Office of the Commercial Counsellor
United States Embassy
24 Grosvenor Square
London W1

Formalities

Foreign investment can be made freely in the USA apart from in designated 'Sensitive' sectors where foreign investment is limited by law. These include communications, airlines, shipping, power generation and mining on Federal lands.

Firms wishing to set up a corporation are required to file with state officials Articles of Incorporation and By-Laws. Registration may take place in any state. Once granted the Certificate of Incorporation, the company may commence business and is generally free to trade in all other states.

There are no restrictions whatsoever on transfers of capital and earnings arising from US investment. Repatriation can take place at any time.

There are no requirements of US participation in the investment, but Sensitive sectors must be US controlled.

When investment takes the form of merger, acquisition or joint venture, the Antitrust Agencies may scrutinise the investment intentions. This applies mainly in cases where each of the firms has substantial market power.

Regional industrialisation incentives

These apply equally to foreign and domestic investors. Each of the 51 states administers its own package of incentives and enquiries should be directed to the respective state capitals or

Regulations, policies and inducements, by country

branch offices in Europe. Addresses are available from the United States Embassy in London.

Federal Government assistance pertains mostly to beneficial tax treatment for new investments. This includes a 7% tax credit for expenditure incurred on plant and machinery, and generous depreciation allowances. Other assistance is more general: infrastructure development, guidance and information services.

Official publications

Invest in the USA, a Federal Government Publication. In addition, most state authorities publish brochures on investment in their areas.

West Germany (Federal Republic of Germany)

Contact ministry

Ministry of Economics in the appropriate *Land* (Federal State) — address available from either of the following:

German Chamber of Industry and Commerce in the UK	Embassy of the Federal Republic of Germany
11 Grosvenor Crescent	23 Belgrave Square
London SW1X 7EE	London SW1X 8P2

Formalities

The setting-up of an overseas subsidiary in West Germany follows the normal procedures established for West German companies. All firms of whatever nationality are required to join and pay annual subscriptions to the Chamber of Commerce in the area they are located.

Regional industrialisation incentives

Financial incentives for new investment are administered and issued by the *Land* (State) Governments. Firms wishing to apply for such assistance should apply to the Ministry of Economics in the appropriate area before any part of the proposed investment is made. Financial assistance varies from area to area but is most generous in West Berlin and the border areas adjacent to East Germany and Czechoslovakia. Other areas outside the agglomeration areas qualify for proportionally less financial assistance. The main categories of assistance are:

1. Investment subsidies of up to 25% of overall investment costs.
2. Government guaranteed loans for periods of 5–10 years at interest rates of 3.5% to 6%.
3. Special accelerated depreciation allowances for plant and machinery.
4. The free of transfer tax purchase of land.
5. The availability of favourable industrial sites.

Official publications

Starting a business in Germany by Dr L. Lotter, German Chamber of Industry and Commerce in the UK; *Guide to Regional Economic Development and Investment Incentive in the Federal Republic of Germany* by Wolfgang Zahn, German Chamber of Industry and Commerce in the UK; *Public Financing Subsidies in the Federal Republic of Germany* by Karlheinz Zahn, Managing Director of the *Hessische Ländesentwicklungsund Treuhandgesellschaft mbH.*; *Establishing a Company in the Federal Republic of Germany*, available from the British Overseas Trade Board Export Services and Promotions Division.

Appendix II UK exchange control policy

All direct investment outward from the UK (except for the 'Scheduled Territories', i.e. the British Isles and Gibraltar) requires the prior approval of Britain's exchange control authorities—the Bank of England acting on behalf of the Treasury—and firms must obtain permission for overseas investment before any part of the investment is made. Exchange controls are not set up to prevent profitable overseas investment *per se*, but to provide the maximum benefit to the UK balance of payments position at the minimum cost to the country's foreign exchange reserves. The controls therefore concern themselves with the methods of financing overseas investment.

When direct investment is to be made in the Overseas Sterling Area or the EEC, permission may be given by the Bank to finance the project entirely from official exchange (that is, foreign currency of the host country purchased at the current market rate in the foreign exchange market) provided that the finance so obtained is employed wholly within those countries.

Otherwise to obtain foreign currency for direct investment overseas at the official rate of exchange, firms are required to promise additional benefits to the UK balance of payments at least equal to the total cost of the investment within eighteen months. These are designated super-criterion projects. These investments may be financed with official exchange to the extent of £250 000 or half the cost of the investment, whichever is the greater. The balance of such investments must be financed either through the investment currency market (where the effective premium varies day-to-day, and since 1972 has varied between 14% and 123%) or by other permitted methods which do not involve an outflow of capital from the UK. The most commonly used method of finance is foreign currency borrowing by the parent company and by the subsidiary under parent guarantee in the host country. Other permitted methods of financing overseas investment include the export free of payment of capital equipment and stock-in-trade of UK manufacture forming an integral part of the investment and the capitalisation of the current account indebtedness.

Investment projects which cannot be classified as super-criterion projects must be financed wholly through the investment currency market or by other methods described in the previous paragraph.

When official permission to invest overseas is sought and given, the Bank will attach conditions to the granting of that permission. Firms are normally required to remit two-thirds of overseas net taxed earnings back to the UK. (This rule, however, does not apply if a majority of the UK parent firm's equity capital is itself foreign owned.)

It is crucial to realise that conditions attached at the time the investment is made are permanent and do not change as official policy is eased or tightened. It is for this reason that firms are recommended to time their overseas investments when the UK balance of payments — which itself is the main influence on the severity of exchange control regulation and implementation — is in relatively good order. Apart from comment given in *The Financial Times* from time to time, the best method of obtaining information is to ask the local branch manager of the firm's normal bank to contact the bank's own foreign exchange department. In addition, firms should watch in the financial sections of newspapers for the 'effective investment premium' or the 'effective conversion factor'. The premium falls and the factor rises as confidence in the future of the pound sterling increases, and this would normally coincide with improving balance of payments and relaxation of exchange control regulation.

Appendix III Questionnaire

NB Identity of the individual firm must not be revealed on this questionnaire.

Can I mention once again that all information given will be confidential, and in the report stage will be unidentifiable with you or your company.

All firms should be asked all questions except where specified.

1. Will you give me a general description of your current products in both the UK and overseas?

2. In what year did your *first* overseas production unit commence operations?

3. In connection with that first foreign investment, in what year did you *first* seek Bank of England permission to invest overseas?

4. How many months was it before you actually received permission from the Bank of England?

5. What was the *single most important* factor that led your firm to make its first foreign investment in production facilities? Classify Answer 5: Push (a); General Pull (b); Specific Pull (b/c).

6. Will you now tell me,

what subsidiary factors were important in that first foreign venture?

7(a) In which country was that investment made?

7(b) Did you in fact locate your plant in (. . .)? Yes (b); No (c).

8(a) Can you identify the single most important factor that led you to select (. . .) as the location for your first overseas production unit?

8(b) Did you look at any alternative countries? Yes/No.

8(c) In which country did you in fact locate your *first* overseas production unit?

9(a) What alternative countries did you look at, before you finally decided to invest in (. . .)?
(1) . . . .   (3) . . . .
(2) . . . .   (4) . . . .

9(b) What alternatives did you look at, before you finally decided to invest in (. . .)?
(1) . . . .   (3) . . . .
(2) . . . .   (4) . . . .

9(c) There was obviously some reason for you preferring (. . .) to (. . .). What was that reason?

10(a) How many months were you seriously considering these alternatives?

10(b) Did you look at other alternative countries as well as (. . .)? Yes/No.
If yes: What alternatives did you look at?
(1) . . . .   (3) . . . .
(2) . . . .   (4) . . . .
How long were you seriously considering these alternatives? . . . months.

11. In which city or province was that first overseas production subsidiary sited? . . .

12. With the benefit of hindsight, what was the *most important* lesson learned?

13. Again with the benefit of hindsight, what was the second most important lesson learned?

14. What was the most serious problem that you encountered in setting up and operating production facilities in (. . .)?

15. What was the second most serious problem that you encountered in setting up and operating production facilities in (. . .)?

16. Has the *actual outcome* of your first overseas venture met the expectations *you* held for it?

17. Has your company made any other foreign investments since the time of the first production venture abroad? Yes/No.
If yes:
(a) In which country(ies) did those subsequent foreign investments take place?
(1). . . . . (2). . . . . (3). . . .
(b) Can you briefly describe those investments?
(c) Why did you choose to invest in [(1), (2), (3) above] rather than expanding your operations in (. . .)?

18. Before the first overseas production subsidiary was established, was *your* firm exporting to (. . .)? Yes/No.

19. When did your firm *first* export to (. . .)?

20. At the time of your first foreign investment were exports to (. . .) a substantial proportion of your production?
(a) above 5% (b) below 5%.

21. Before *that* production unit was established, had your firm *ever* had an agent or a sales subsidiary in (. . .)?
YES: agent/sales subsidiary;
NO: agent/sales subsidiary.
(Delete where inapplicable.)
If yes:
(a) When was the agent appointed? (b) When was the sales subsidiary set up?

22. At the time of *that* first foreign investment did *your* firm have supply sources in (. . .) for (a) raw materials, and (b) intermediate goods?
(a) for raw materials: Yes/No; (b) for intermediate goods: Yes/No.

23. Did your main UK competitors have interests in (. . .) at that time? Yes/No.
If yes:
(a) Were they exporting to (. . .) at that time? Yes/No;
(b) Did they have production facilities in (. . .)? Yes/No.

24. Can you describe the *business* and *personal* contacts that *you* and your colleagues had in (. . .) immediately prior to that first production venture overseas taking place?

25. Considering now the links and contacts that you have mentioned above, how

important were these in the overall decision to invest in (. . .)?

(26.) Again considering the links and contacts that you have mentioned above, how important have they proved subsequently in the success of your venture?

27. Before the investment decision was taken, who went to (. . .) on the firm's behalf and what did they do there?

28. What was the single most important *piece* of information required about the (. . .) market, other than accumulated experience, before you took the final decision?

29. Can you now tell me what was the single most important *source* of information regarding what the firm wanted to know about (. . .)?

30. What other sources contributed to information?

31. Before the first foreign investment took place, did your company become involved in market research activities in (. . .)? Yes/No. *If yes:* What form of activities?

32. Before you took your final decision to invest in (. . .) did you investigate any inducements offered by the (. . .) government?

33. What inducements did you take up?

34. How important in the overall decision to invest in (. . .) were these inducements?
(i) very important; (ii) important; (iii) a bonus; (iv) insignificant.

35. When you *first* decided to invest in (. . .), what *kind* of investment did you want to make?
(i) greenfield venture; (ii) majority of an existing firm's equity; (iii) minority stake in an existing firm.

36. Why did you prefer *that type* of investment?

37. In the outcome, what type of investment did you make?
(i) greenfield; (ii) majority; (iii) minority.

If answer 37 is different from answer 35:

38. What was responsible for you changing the original 'mode' of investment?

Acquisition firms only:

39. Did you have any personal or trading contacts with the (. . .) firm before the acquisition? Yes/No.
If yes:
(i) Can you describe the form of this contact?
(ii) Would you have gone ahead with your investment if you had not had the links and contacts mentioned above?
(iii) With the benefit of hindsight, do you think that you acquired the 'right' company?
If no:
(i) How did you select the company that you acquired in the absence of links and contacts?
(ii) With the benefit of hindsight, do you think that you selected the 'right' company this way?

40. What was the single most important factor in choosing (. . .) as the site for the firm's production unit?

41. Can you describe the production that was *initially* carried out in (. . .)?

42. At that time, how did *you* decide *which* of your products to produce in the (. . .) plant?

43. In the *first* year of operations in the (. . .) plant was the 'bought-in' component of production mainly imported or was it mainly purchased in (. . .)?
(i) mainly imported: from UK/from elsewhere; (ii) mainly purchased in (. . .).

44. In the *current* year of production in the (. . .) plant has the source of the 'bought-in' component changed?
(i) mainly imported: from UK/from elsewhere; (ii) mainly purchased in (. . .).

45. On balance and with the benefit of hindsight, do you think that you 'did the best thing' by investing in (. . .) rather than in one of the other countries you mentioned earlier?

46. Given that you have competitors in (. . .), at what level of the consumer market do you orientate your sales promotion activities?
(i) high price 'luxury' end of market; (ii) 'middle' market price range; (iii) mass market 'low' price range.

47. With the benefit of hindsight, knowing what you know now, do *you* think that *this* was the 'correct' marketing strategy for your firm?

48. Is it the same strategy that you follow in the UK?

49. Who are your main competitors in (. . .)?
(i) main UK rivals; (ii) other UK firms; (iii) other overseas firms; (iv) indigenous firms.

50. With the benefit of hindsight, do *you* think that *your* company should have 'gone' where competition is different?

51. Before you commenced production in (. . .), what objectives did you set for the overseas subsidiary in terms of performance?

52. In the actual outcome, how did the *results* of overseas production compare with your objectives?

53. Looking purely at financial objectives, were your targets set in any of the following ways:
(i) rate of return on book assets; (ii) positive cash flow after . . . years. How many years? (iii) DCF of expected time stream of earnings. What discount rate did you use?

54. In terms of financial targets, were you expecting a higher rate of return on your overseas investment than you expect on your UK investments?

55. In the *current* year, how does performance overseas compare with that in the UK in terms of profitability?
(i) overseas more profitable; (ii) UK more profitable; (iii) about the same.

56. In general policy terms and given the choice, would you reinvest profits in the (. . .) subsidiary, or would you prefer to remit them to the UK? reinvest/remit.

57. Can you give me a rough estimate of the proportion of profits reinvested in the (. . .) subsidiary since operations began in (. . .)?

58. What criteria do you use in the decision to reinvest or remit profits from (. . .)?

59. Has the profit remitted

Appendix III

to the UK since operations began in (. . .) exceeded the initial investment outlay from the UK?

60. Is the (. . .) subsidiary responsible for a part of the group's research and development programme? Yes/No.
If yes: In what area does it concentrate its activities?

61. Is the subsidiary responsible for its own marketing?

62. Is the subsidiary responsible for its own purchasing?

63. Is the subsidiary responsible for its own labour training?

64. Is any charge made to the (. . .) subsidiary for its share of parent company overheads?

65. Are royalties or management fees charged to the subsidiary?

66. How do you set the price at which you invoice the subsidiary for materials and components sent from the UK?

67. Is this the same as for any other overseas customer?

68. Is the chief executive of the (. . .) subsidiary a member of the main UK board?

69. What is the *maximum* size of any capital investment project that the local board can ratify at the present time without reference to the UK board? £. . .

70. How often does your overseas subsidiary submit (a) budget estimates and (b) accounts to the UK in the *current* year?
(a) budget estimates . . . months; (b) accounts . . . months.

71. Can the local board raise any of the following without reference to the UK board?
(i) prices; (ii) wages; (iii) levels of advertising expenditure.

72. In the *current* year, is the local board responsible for management recruitment in (. . .)? Yes/No.

73. What nationality is the chief executive of your (. . .) subsidiary?
(i) British (ii) (. . .) (iii) other.

74. Can you quickly compare what you have just described to me, with the activities of

your UK subsidiaries (if you have any)?

75. Have you expanded your operations in (. . .) since your first foreign investment took place? Yes/No.
If yes: Can we conclude from this that you *entered* (. . .) at too small a scale?

76. Have you any plans to expand the scale of operations in (. . .)?

77. Since production began in (. . .), have this company's exports to (. . .):
(i) increased; (ii) remained the same; (iii) declined.

78. Similarly, since production began in (. . .), have this company's imports to the UK from (. . .):
(i) increased; (ii) remained the same; (iii) declined.

79. With the benefit of hindsight, knowing what you know now, how would you do it differently if you were setting about it today?

80. In the current year:
(a) how many people do you employ in the UK? (b) how many people do you employ in (. . .)?

81. In the last completed financial year, what was the:
(a) sales turnover of UK operations? (b) sales turnover of (. . .) operations?

Index

Accounts, 127-8, 148
   success ratings, 127
Advertising,
   expenditure control, 133
   France, 31
Age of subsidiaries, 18
Agents, see Foreign agents
Audit fees,
   Italy, 155
Australia,
   capital expenditure, 131
   closures and sales, 166, 167
   engineering industry, 131
   functional control, 134
   government regulations, policies and inducements, 204-7
   joint ventures, 72-3
   labour shortage, 173
   market sectors, 101
   nationality of chief executive, 138
   second and subsequent ventures, 173
   success ratings, 62
   tariff barriers, 22, 33, 53
Automation, 31

Back to back loans, 119, 121

Bahamas,
   overseas sales subsidiaries, 163
Bank of England, 119-22, 124-5, 141, 229-31
Belgium,
   closures and sales, 32, 53
   government regulations, policies and inducements, 207-9
   imports to UK, 147
   joint ventures, 33-4, 72
   language problems, 156
   second and subsequent ventures, 163
   success ratings, 62
   transport costs, 33
Bribes, 73
Budget estimates, 127-8

Canada,
   government regulations, policies and inducements, 209-11
   overseas sales subsidiaries, 163
   second and subsequent ventures, 163
Capital expenditure, 129-31
   Netherlands, 129
   overseas sales subsidiaries, 195

success ratings, 130
Capital investment, 38, 39, 112, 141
Capital losses, 29-30, 32, 40
Chief executives, 137-9, 150
　nationality, 31, 33, 137-8, 158
　success ratings, 137
　overseas sales subsidiaries, 196-7
　selection, 158, 173
　see also Managers
Civil servants, 73
Closures and sales, 26, 29-34
　Australia, 166, 167
　Belgium, 32, 53
　France, 29, 30
　Italy, 29, 30
　South Africa, 31-2
Cologne, 39, 115
Commercial banks, 88
Communications problems,
　chief executive, 137
　distance, 31, 33, 135, 153
　　overseas sales subsidiaries, 195
　language, 64, 156
Competitors, 86
　see also Foreign competitors
Control procedures, 126-51
　chief executive, 137-9
　compared with UK subsidiaries, 135-7, 150
　financial, 127-32, 148
　financial policies, 139-44, 150
　functional, 132-5, 149-50
　intra-firm trade, 144-9, 150
　overseas production subsidiaries, 194-7
Control strategy, see Ownership strategy
Customs regulations, 142

Decision making, 132-5
Desk research, 85, 89, 91
Development areas, 116-7
Discounted cash flow, 111
Dishonesty, 32

Dollar premium, 120

EEC,
　financial risk, 64
　markets, 33, 38, 57, 60, 64-5
　overseas sales subsidiaries, 163
　second and subsequent ventures, 163
　success ratings, 62-3
Electronics industry,
　West Germany, 115
Employees, see Labour force
　see also Chief executive; Managers
Engineering industry, 49, 129
　Australia, 131
　Ireland, 118
Equity holdings, 39, 134
Establishment of subsidiaries,
　motivating factors, 51-2, 54-9
　outside stimuli, 54
　planning, 65-97
　strategy for success, 66-7
　tariff barriers, 52-4
Exchange, see Foreign exchange
Exports from UK, 26-9, 43, 44, 47, 102, 148
　via overseas sales subsidiaries, growth, 180-3
　previous experience, 190-2
　see also Intra-firm trade; Imports to UK

Factories, see Premises
Failures, 22, 26, 29-34
Financial control, 127-32
　accounts, 127-8, 148
　　success ratings, 127
　budget estimates, 127-8, 148
　　success ratings, 127
　capital expenditure, 129-31
　lessons learned, 156
　problems, 173-4
Financial inducements, 118-9
　overseas sales subsidiaries, 194

Index

see also Government regulations, policies and inducements
Financial objectives, 111-12
  success ratings, 112
Financial policies, 139-44, 150
  management services, 140
  profits, 139-40
  royalty payments, 140
  transfer pricing, 142-4
Financial risk, 2, 16-19, 25, 64, 72-3, 109, 112, 121
Firms participating, see Parent firms
Foreign agents, 44, 47, 60, 113-14
Foreign competitors, 87, 89, 102, 143, 155, 188
  Australia, 166
  France, 189
Foreign exchange, 72, 107
  control, 119-22, 124-5, 142, 229-31
  time taken, 120
  profit forecasts, 121
  profits, 140
France,
  advertising, 31
  closures and sales, 29, 30
  government regulations, policies and inducements, 211-13
  overseas sales subsidiaries, 163
  second and subsequent ventures, 163
  success rating, 62
Frankfurt, 40, 115
Functional control, 132-5, 149-50
  autonomy, 136
  success ratings, 133, 134

Government regulations, policies and inducements, 84, 86, 92, 116-19, 202-28
  financial, 118-19
  overseas sales subsidiaries, 194
  success ratings, 116-19, 124
  see also, names of individual countries (listed under 'Host countries')
Growth
  overseas production subsidiaries, 22-4
  overseas sales subsidiaries, 184-7

Heavy metals industry, 72, 147
Holland, see Netherlands
Host countries,
  business practices, 21, 31, 137
  civil servants, 73
  commonwealth countries, 64
  government inducements, 84, 86, 92, 116-19, 202-8
  labour force, 92, 114, 115, 117
  sales methods, 20-1
  selection, 59-61
  success ratings, 62-5
  trading blocs, 63
  visits, 91-4
  see also, Australia; Bahamas; Belgium; Canada; EEC; France; India; Ireland; Italy; Luxembourg; Malta; Mexico; Netherlands; New Zealand; Nigeria; Norway; Portugal; South Africa; Spain; Sweden; USA; West Germany

Import quotas, 53
Imports to UK, 146-7, 168
India,
  second and subsequent ventures, 163
Insurance costs, 159
Intra-firm trade, 144-9, 150
  exports from UK, 148
  raw materials, 144-5
  sales to UK, 146-7
Investing stages, 98-125
  financial objectives, 111
  foreign exchange control, 119-22

government inducements, 116-19,
  202-28
marketing strategy, 99-103
overseas sales subsidiary, 192-4
performance objectives, 108-13
  success ratings, 109
pre-investment steps, 43-51
  success ratings, 46, 48-51
pricing strategy, 99-103
product policy, 103-8
site selection, 113-5
  success ratings, 114
Investment currency market, 119, 231
Investment information, 96, 230-1
Ireland, 62
  functional control, 135
  government regulations, policies and inducements, 118, 213-14
  imports to UK, 147
  second and subsequent ventures, 163
Italy,
  closures and sales, 29, 30
  local conditions and culture, 155
  success ratings, 62

Joint ventures, 73
  Belgium, 34, 72
    problems, 157
  Mexico, 167
    problems, 173

Labour force, 92, 114, 115, 117
  costs, 159
  numbers, 13, 169-70
  shortages, 172
  turnover, 173
Labour intensive production, 116
Language problems, 64, 138
  Belgium, 156
  France, 31
Leisure market, 38
Lessons learned, 81-2, 152-78

problems encountered, 171-6, 177
second and subsequent ventures, 161-8, 177
size and ownership of subsidiaries, 169-70, 177
Licensing agreements, 22, 25
Location of premises, 113-15
  success ratings, 114, 123-4
Losses, 29-30, 32, 40
  Belgium, 109
Luxembourg
  government regulations, policies and inducements, 214-16
  labour shortages, 173
  success ratings, 38, 62

Malta
  exports to UK, 168
  second and subsequent ventures, 163
Management services, 140
Managers
  chief executives, 137-9
  dishonesty, 32
  foreign nationals, 39, 40, 73, 80-1, 101
    success ratings, 134-5
  professionalism, 156
  recruitment, 133
  training, 39
  UK nationals, 39, 40, 80-1
Managing directors, see Chief executives
Manufacturing processes, 104-5
Market research, 84-5, 88-91
  agencies, 89, 90
  lessons learned, 166
Market share, 53, 110
  Australia, 166, 167
Marketing strategy, 99-103
  control, 133
  failures, 102
  lessons learned, 158-9, 168
  market segments, 100, 122

Index

market share, 108, 109
problems, 174
success ratings, 100
Mexico, 26
joint ventures, 167
overseas sales subsidiaries, 163
technology, 166
Multinational companies, 33, 53

Nationalism, 38, 138
Netherlands
budget estimates, 129
government regulations, policies and inducements, 216-18
marketing strategy, 103
reasons for selection, 61
second and subsequent ventures, 163
success ratings, 62
takeovers, 39, 49
New products, 38, 168
New Zealand
closures and sales, 167
government regulations, policies and inducements, 218-20
second and subsequent ventures, 163
Nigeria
second and subsequent ventures, 163
Norway
government regulations, policies and inducements, 220-22
second and subequent ventures, 53, 163
success ratings, 62

Objectives, 21-22
see also, Performance objectives
Overheads, 17
Overseas countries, see Host countries
Overseas sales subsidiaries, 2, 8, 40, 44, 47, 179-97
chief executives, 196
control procedures, 194-7, 198
expansion, 184-7
expectations and objectives, 183-4
exports,
growth, 180-3, 198
previous experience, 190-2
location, 163
planning and investment, 192-4, 198
reasons for establishing, 188-90, 198
success ratings, 190
second and subsequent ventures, 25, 163
Overseas Sterling Area, 119
Overseas visits, 91-4
objectives, 91-2
success ratings, 93
Ownership strategy, 70-4, 169-70
joint ventures, 73
one-hundred-percent control, 72-3
success ratings, 71
takeovers v. greenfield ventures, 74-8
success ratings, 77-8, 170

Parent firms, 2-4, 6-13
criteria for selection, 6-8
date of establishment, 41-2
international outlook, 167
lessons learned, 81-2, 152-78
number of employees, 12
ownership, 10-11
problems, 175
sales turnover, 11-12
size, 41-2, 169-70, 177
Standard Industrial Classification, 8-10
takeovers, 11
technology intensity, 41-2
Performance objectives, 19-22, 108-13
financial, 111

overseas sales subsidiaries, 183-4
  success ratings, 109, 123
Personnel management, 39
Planning, 65-97
  lessons learned, 81-2
  market research, 84-5, 88-91
  overseas sales subsidiaries, 192-4
  overseas visits, 91-4
  ownership strategy, 70-4
    success ratings, 71
    takeovers v. greenfield ventures, 74-8
    success ratings, 77-8
Portugal,
  second and subsequent ventures, 163
Pre-investment steps, 43-51
  success ratings, 46, 48-51
Premises,
  construction, 31, 38
  labour force, 117
  site selection, 113-15
    success ratings, 114, 123-4
Pricing strategy, 30, 31, 99-103
  control, 133
  lessons learned, 158-9
  market segments, 100
  overseas sales subsidiaries, 187
  success ratings, 100
  transfer pricing, 18, 142-4
Problems encountered, 171-6, 177
Product policy, 38, 65, 75, 101, 103-8
  lessons learned, 158-9
  success ratings, 104, 123
Production capacity, 24, 32
Production levels, 107
Production methods, 31, 104-5
Professional management, 156
Profitability, 16-19, 35, 40, 50, 111, 121
Profits policy, 139-42
Purchasing policy
  control, 133

raw materials, 144-5

Quality control, 30, 31, 135
  lessons learned, 156
  problems, 174
Questionnaire, 232-9

Race relations
  South Africa, 156
Raw materials, 143, 144-5
  supply problems, 174
Recruitment control, 133
Redundancy payments, 159
Regional policies, 116-17
Re-investment policies, 140-1
Research and development, 133, 134
Research interviews, 2-4
  questionnaire, 232-9
Return on investments, 112, 141
Risk, 64, 108, 138, 201
  see also, Financial risk
Royalty payments, 140

Sales methods, 20-1, 30
Sales promotion, 100, 174
Sales to UK, 146-7, 168
Sales turnover, 13, 33, 38, 48-50, 169-70
Scheduled Territories, 119
Second and subsequent ventures, 24-6, 161-8, 177
  foreign exchange controls, 121
  location, 163
  overseas sales subsidiaries, 163, 185
  success ratings, 162
  technology, 166
Selection of host country, 59-61
Silver plating industry, 135
Site selection, 113-15
  success ratings, 114, 123-4
Size of parent firm, 41-2, 169-70
  success ratings, 170
South Africa,
  closures and sales, 31-2

Index

government regulations, policies and inducements, 222-4
nationality of chief executive, 138
overseas sales subsidiaries, 163
quality control, 156
race relations, 156
second and subsequent ventures, 163
success ratings, 39, 62
tariff barriers, 50, 53
Spain,
second and subsequent ventures, 163
Staff, see Labour force
see also Chief executive; Managers
Standard Industrial Classification, 8-10
Strikes, 31, 172
Subsidiary companies, see Overseas sales subsidiaries
Success overall,
overseas production subsidiaries, 19-22, 199-201
ratings, 34-40
technology intensity, 41-2
overseas sales subsidiaries, 187-8, 197
Sweden,
government regulations, policies and inducements, 224-7

Takeovers,
overseas sales subsidiaries, 193-4
product policy, 105-6
site selection, 113
v. greenfield ventures, 74-8
success ratings, 77-8
Tariff barriers, 33, 50, 52-3
Tax regulations, 142, 174
Technology, 41-2, 166, 167
Theft, 32

Trade, see Exports from UK; Intra-firm trade; Imports to UK; Sales to UK
Trade unions, 56
Trading blocs, 63-4, 164-5
Training,
control, 133
managers, 39
problems, 172, 173
Transfer pricing, 18, 142-4
intra-firm trade, 142, 144-9
success ratings, 143
Transport costs, 33, 56, 92, 135
raw materials, 146

UK subsidiaries, 135-7
USA,
government regulations, policies and inducements, 226-7
local conditions and culture, 155
markets, 168
product specifications, 57
second and subsequent ventures, 163
success ratings, 20-1, 26, 27, 62
technology, 166

Wages,
control, 133
costs, 159
West Germany,
closures and sales, 32
competitors, 156
foreign exchange control, 121
government regulations, policies and inducements, 227-8
greenfield ventures, 75
reasons for selection, 49, 54, 56, 61
site selection, 115
success ratings, 27, 29, 38, 39-40, 62